WHEN GOD IS YOUR FATHER

Everything Changes

LEE CUMMINGS

The author has tried to recreate events and conversations from his memories of them. To maintain their anonymity in some instances, names and identifying details have been changed to protect the privacy of individuals.

While the author has made every effort to provide accurate internet addresses at the time of publication, neither the publisher nor the author assumes any responsibility for errors or for changes that occur after publication. Further, the publisher does not have any control over and does not assume any responsibility for author or third-party websites or their content.

I am dedicating this book to a man who has been a spiritual father to me throughout most of my adult life and even before that. Pastor Loren Covarrubias has modeled what it means to know God as Father and encouraged me in every season of my maturity and development. We have a thousand teachers but not many fathers. I am eternally grateful for his steady voice cheering me on all these years. Thank you.

Contents

I am no longer an orphan.
I am no longer alone.
I've been adopted.
I've been accepted.
My heart has found a home.

Your Spirit's living within me.
You tend to wounds in my soul.
'Cause I've been adopted.
I've been accepted.
My heart has found a home.

I am Your child; You are my Father.
All that I need is found right here with You.

Your love came running to meet me,
Your grace deeper than the sea.
All that I've longed for is found in You, Father.
My heart has found a home.

You found me when I wandered far.
You held me close; You healed my heart.

You gave me life, called me by name.
Now I'm alive, set free and safe.

You never leave through joy and pain.
You raised me up, showed me Your grace.
In every change, You have been true.
All of my life belongs to You.

"Right Here With You" by Radiant City Music

The lyrics above are from an EP containing three songs—"Father's Love," "Right Here With You," and "Amazed By Your Love." The EP was created to echo the heart behind this book. Each song is meant to give language and melody to the truths found in the following pages, helping you not only understand the love of the Father, but also experience it. Our prayer is that, as you read and listen, the message would sink even deeper into your heart—that through both word and song, you encounter the steady, pursuing, faithful love of the Father. Scan the QR code below to listen to these songs.

Chapter 1
Leaving Behind the Fractured Image

Perched on the front steps of our rented house in Pontiac, Michigan, I sat waiting for my father's arrival. I was an excited kid looking forward to spending time with my dad. The only problem was my dad moved through my life like an unpredictable cold wind.

Would he come this time? Would he remember that he promised to pick me up before dark?

Waiting for what seemed like forever to my four-year-old self, I jumped to my feet whenever I heard a car coming down the road, thinking—hoping—it was my dad. But I was disappointed each time. One car, a pickup truck, another car, and still no Dad. At some point, the thought that he might not come started to overshadow my soul, so I stopped getting up to see if the vehicle I heard rumbling down the road belonged to him. My eyes kept watch, nonetheless.

After a while, the sun finally went down. The streetlights came on. Mom came over and sat beside me, but Dad was nowhere around. Like the *wah-wah-wah,* muted trombone sounds of adult speech animated in a Charlie Brown movie, she said something to me, took my hand, and pulled me up and toward the front door. I knew this meant my dad wasn't coming, and then I clearly heard her say, "It's time to come inside and get ready for bed," words no kid ever wants to hear.

Conflicted and confused, I resisted going inside, holding on to the thought that, if I waited a little longer, Dad would somehow materialize. I pulled away from my mother to look one last time but soon followed her inside, hurt and dejected.

Unfortunately, this pattern repeated itself countless times in my childhood, teaching me one of my earliest life lessons: My father was not someone I could depend on.

My Four Fathers

My parents' relationship had developed when they were kids and were living around the corner from each other. It eventually led to their marriage when they were still in their teens. In fact, Michael "Mickey" Cummings married my mother, Donna, when he was eighteen. Both struggled to find equilibrium in life, and both imported family pain into their marriage. Ultimately, Dad abandoned Mom and me in the inner city of Pontiac a few years later. He was twenty, Mom twenty-one, and me nine months old.

My biological father was an example of an absent and untrustworthy father. A prodigal father, if you will. By the grace of God, he encountered Jesus and received salvation later in life. He and I developed a fantastic relationship as a result, and he became an amazing grandfather to my children. As a child, however, I needed a father, and my dad just wasn't there. The pain of his absence and rejection left an indelible mark upon my young soul.

When I was seven, my mom remarried, bringing into my life a stepfather who was present but seemed emotionally unavailable. He was a good provider and disciplinarian. He had a strong moral code, teaching me the importance of having integrity and a good work ethic. What I liked most was how he took good care of my mother. The only problem was I felt as if I were a subsidy that he had to finance, a mistake from my mom's past that he had to shoulder.

Over the years, he and I have strengthened our relationship, and I have a deep appreciation for him. Of course, I now understand how difficult it must have been for my stepfather. After all, what chance did he have of replacing my biological father in my eyes? Absolutely none. Yet his was a thankless task, especially when I was too young to appreciate what he did and tried to do for me. All this meant was I didn't have the closeness that I'd longed for with my dad or my stepfather throughout my childhood, adolescent, and teen years. I was left to wonder, *What's wrong with me? Why doesn't anyone want to be my father?*

Thankfully, I did have a grandfather who was present in my life and was the one who taught me to love Jesus. He became a surrogate father to me. In many ways, he spoke identity over me. He read the Bible to me, played catch with me, and picked me up on the weekends, taking me to church with him and my grandmother. My grandfather, more than anything, pointed me toward my fourth father, my Heavenly Father.

At the age of twelve, my Heavenly Father encountered me tenderly, spoke my name, and told me what my purpose was. That day, He initiated the years-long process of healing the deep wounds of fatherlessness in my soul. He also began to reveal Himself to me, not only as my Creator, but as the One who knew me before I even took my first breath, the One who called me, the

One who loved me so much He sent His one and only Son to save and rescue me.

Regrettably, my teen years were far from perfect years. I struggled. Mine was the testimony of a broken young man who, by all accounts, should have been a statistic yet was redeemed by my Heavenly Father who never gave up hope. He stood at the end of the road, like the father in the parable of the prodigal son, waiting for me to come home. And when I did, He embraced me, welcomed me into His family, and made a place for me at His table.

The Fatherless Epidemic

Mine isn't the only life impacted by the sporadic presence or total absence of a father. Perhaps, yours is too. Sadly, many children in America today are growing up in fatherless homes. Indeed, we're experiencing *a fatherless epidemic* in our country, and it's not going unnoticed by religious, social, and governmental institutions.

On Father's Day in June of 2025, for example, three GOP lawmakers from the 119th Congress introduced House Resolution 487, more commonly known as the *Fatherhood Resolution.*[1] The statement issued by the House of Representatives recognized the important role a father plays in the nurture and development of his children and also cited the negative impact his absence can have on the lives of the same. The data available at the time of this book's publication is telling.

According to the US Census Bureau, one in four children in America live without a father in the home.[2] That's 18.4 million children.[3] The world average for children raised by a single parent is 7 percent. The average for children raised by a single parent in

America is 23 percent, which is the highest rate of any country on the planet.[4] Furthermore, "fathers are absent in approximately 80 percent of single-parent homes."[5] Moreover, 40 percent of children that are born today are born out of wedlock.[6]

The real-life impact that fatherlessness is having in the US is as staggering as it is pervasive:

- 90 percent of runaway and homeless youth are from fatherless homes.

- 85 percent of children involved in the juvenile court system are from fatherless homes.

- 71 percent of high school dropouts are from fatherless homes.

- 65 percent of children who live below the poverty line are from fatherless homes.

- 50 percent of youth who commit suicide are from fatherless homes.[7]

These statistics tell us in no uncertain terms that fatherlessness wounds the spirit and soul of children and youth. We know it even can have calamitous results for generations, becoming as it has for America a societal problem.

The Church and Fatherlessness

At its core, fatherlessness is a spiritual problem. We could even say it's a sin issue that goes all the way back to the garden of Eden.

There, Adam and Eve ate fruit from the forbidden Tree of the Knowledge of Good and Evil. We're told later in the New Testament that Eve was deceived by Satan but Adam ate knowingly.[8] Their sinful act, then, was rebellion against God. And in their sin, they rejected God as their Heavenly Father. Their rejection resulted in us all being alienated from God the Father and living under the curse of sin and death until we were redeemed back to Him through the sacrificial gift of the Son of God. We find restoration through faith in His Son, Jesus Christ.

God wants us to know Him as our Father, and that's not only a fundamental, foundational understanding of who God is, but it's also one of the most difficult and, I believe, one of the most broken revelations within the Body of Christ. As we've seen, the image of fatherhood is fractured in our world today, and that has greatly impacted how we view the Fatherhood of God. We need a fresh revelation of who God our Father is, and the most perfect revelation of God as Father is seen in Jesus, His Son.

The spiritual wound of broken relationship with God the Father is gaping within the Church. *In fact, many in the Church have not yet come to the full heart revelation of what it means for God to be their Father, and it's adversely affecting the overall health and order of the Church.*

How do I know this to be true? As a pastor, I witness men, women, and young people who continue to struggle with what others have termed *an orphan spirit, an orphan mentality,* or *an orphan heart.* Put simply, they're living as if they're fatherless. Their lives evidence the fear, shame, guilt, and self-protection of those who don't experientially know God as their Father. And all this is further manifested in their hiding, masking, withdrawing, and isolating. It grieves me to say how often I have even seen sons and daughters of God struggle with issues of identity and self-worth, things I've struggled with myself in my spiritual journey. All the while, God the Father is wanting us to receive the life, provision, protection, identity, and direction He has for us.

What about you? If your earthly beginnings were anything like mine, then you know all too well what it's like to experience biological or spiritual fatherlessness. But even if you have had a very present and loving earthly father, and were raised in a spiritually vibrant family, that doesn't necessarily mean you've come to fully know God as your Father.

No matter your family of origin—no matter your present relationship with your earthly father—you have a Heavenly Father who, from before time began, has desired for you to be a member of His family. I want that to sink down into the deepest parts of your heart like a soothing balm. You are wanted. You are welcome. You belong. You matter.

Before you even existed on Earth, beloved, God the Father planned and designed for you to be His child. It bears repeating that He has longed for you to be in His family. His heart for you is that you would come to know and experience Him more and more as your ever-present, faithful, gracious, benevolent, and loving Father.

The Fatherhood of God

Here's the reality about who God is. From the very beginning, God has been a father. It wasn't something that He tried to become. Neither was His the mere benevolent behavior of a distant deity. He didn't become a father when He created the angels or humanity. Neither did He become a father when He sent Jesus to the earth. *God is, was, and always has been Father.* And can I tell you that He is the perfect Father?

While we earthly dads try to come to the measure of the fullness of being good fathers, God hasn't ever had to *try* to be good. He always has been good—eternally good. Not only is God good, but 1 John 4:8 tells us, "God is love." The Fatherhood, goodness, and love of God express His being relational while pointing to another truth, and that is this: *God always has existed and dwelt in community and family.* God the Father, God the Son, and God the Holy Spirit are three Persons within the Godhead who have eternally coexisted together as One in perfect community and perfect love. As one theologian has written:

> From all eternity, the Father speaks the Son, who is a perfect image of the Father; the Son and the Father look at one another and they fall in love. The love that they breathe back and forth is the *Spiritus Sanctus,* literally "the holy breath."[9]

God can't be described as love if there is no other being or person in the universe to whom He can express that love. If God were a singular, unitarian God without Father, Son, and Holy Spirit, how could God be eternally relational, how could God be eternally good, and how could He be eternally love?

So, when we look at God eternally being Father, we must conclude that He always has lived in community within a family—Father, Son, and Holy Spirit. At some point in eternity past, the Godhead made angels and heavenly beings. But then, the Godhead decided to create a world in which the Father, Son, and Holy Spirit could relate to and have a loving relationship with not only heavenly beings, but with beings resembling Himself, beings made with the capacity for relationship with Him and made to be like Him. Hence, the Godhead said, "Let us make man in our

image, after our likeness."[10] And God created male and female—
He created us—to be in His family. God created us out of a desire
to love and to be loved in return. Yet, when God created us, He
made us with the ability to choose or deny His love. He took a
great risk, giving us the right of refusal. *For love to be real and true,
there must be the right of refusal, the ability to say* no *to the offer.*

God, in His infinite wisdom and in His infinite power and
strength, created human beings for the purpose of having a family.
In the manifold wisdom and glory of God, He planned a way to
show His great love and win the hearts of men, women, young
people, and children throughout the generations, one day deliv-
ering them out of the mess and chaos their initial refusal of that
love created.

> But when the time arrived that was set by God the Father,
> God sent his Son, born among us of a woman, born under
> the conditions of the law so that he might redeem those of
> us who have been kidnapped by the law. Thus we have
> been set free to experience our rightful heritage. You can
> tell for sure that you are now fully adopted as his own chil-
> dren because God sent the Spirit of his Son into our lives
> crying out, "Papa! Father!" Doesn't that privilege of inti-
> mate conversation with God make it plain that you are not
> a slave, but a child? And if you are a child, you're also an
> heir, with complete access to the inheritance.
>
> — Galatians 4:4–7 The Message

And yet we've forgotten, we've run, and we've hidden behind
religion, much like a broken and rebellious Adam and Eve hiding
from God behind fig leaves and the trees of the garden when He

came pursuing them. Because of this, because of our reckless living, it takes the Father to teach us what it means to be a son or daughter—to put His Spirit in us to teach us to say, "Abba, Father," and relate to God as Father. As John the Beloved rightly expressed, "Behold what manner of love the Father has bestowed upon us, that we should be called children of God!"[11]

Beloved, if Jesus Christ is your Lord and Savior, then God is your Father. And He doesn't want you only to have head knowledge of that truth. He wants you to live your life as His child with all the full benefits and inheritance as His heir. He wants you to both know and experience His fatherly care and affection. He doesn't want you talking about Him as Father while not living in the life-changing reality of His being Abba, Father, to you. God wants to heal the wounds and the scars of both biological and spiritual fatherlessness.

In the following chapters, we're going to zero in on what it means to know God as Father. Each chapter will start with some type of memory from my childhood, adolescent, or teen years. These are broken reflections of my experiences meant to encourage you to address some of what might be similar fractures found in your own life. Please know the Father has healed my heart throughout the years and has transformed what was fractured and shattered into something beautiful. I trust He will do the same for you. Also, I've included prayer and reflection sections at the end of each chapter to help you engage and dive deeper into the topics of each chapter. My goal is to address what wounds in our hearts need to be healed even now, even if we're in Christ, so that we can rightly relate to our Heavenly Father. Along the way, we will discover what it means to belong to the Father, to be adopted by Him, and to be orphaned no more. Everything changes in your life when you begin to *know* God as Father.

Prayer

Father, today, we ask for Your help because only You can heal the wounds of our fatherlessness. Only You can heal the wounds of our brokenness, the wounds caused by our earthly fathers or by their absence. Maybe we had great fathers, yet we struggle with believing that You will still be at the end of the road, looking for us to come home, in spite of our misses, messes, and misgivings.

Holy Spirit, I pray that You teach us how to say, "Abba," how to say, "Papa," with knowledge and conviction that nothing can separate us from the Father's love, that our names are written in the palms of Jesus's hands, that the Father's eyes are on us for good and not for evil, and that, even though we've bankrupted our emotional inheritance, He's able to restore.

Father, teach us how to love You back. And thank You for bringing us to our senses in the pigpens of our lives. Though our sin, guilt, and shame have seemed overwhelming, thank You for welcoming us home and into Your family.

Reflection

1. Can you think of a time in your childhood when you felt let down or disappointed by a father figure? How did that impact or shape your life?

2. Who has been the most influential father figure in your life? What did you learn from him about love, trust, or identity?

3. A.W. Tozer said, "What comes into our minds when we think about God is the most important thing about us."[12] What do you think about God? How does that affect the way you relate to Him?

4. In what ways have you experienced God as Father?

5. What one insecurity or hurt would you like the love of your Heavenly Father to heal?

Chapter 2
Looking to the Perfect Image

Tuned in to channel 17 WXMI, the TV stood ready, powered on with commercials blaring. It was almost six o'clock in the evening, and that meant three things: (1) The grandfather clock in our family living room would soon announce the hour; (2) I'd see my stepfather's car lights shine through the window as he turned into the driveway, reminding me I'd probably be in trouble when he came inside; and (3) my favorite TV show would begin.

When the grandfather clock began to sound its sixteen-note Westminster Chimes, I saw the car lights. Then, the hammer of the clock began its successive six strokes announcing the hour. And as though through some magical synchronicity, the iconic four solo notes of the familiar French horn sounded from the TV. I reacted to those notes as if a bugler were calling reveille, so I ran fast to line up only a foot or two away from the TV screen. My adolescent eyes fixed immediately on the screen, watching the covered wagon draw closer and closer and loom larger and larger before me.

Soon, the full orchestra echoed the French horn's introduction as the music's pace picked up and the picture cut to a close-up of Charles and Caroline Ingalls, sitting in the wagon's box seat, both smiling like all get-out. Next came their children in birth order—Mary, Laura, and Carrie Ingalls—each one running down the grassy hill along with their scruffy dog Jack, Carrie tumbling on her way. They were all heading to what I knew to be their "little house on the prairie."

I was glued to the images before me, but the one face that held my attention was that of Charles. He was "Pa" to his girls and a perfect father figure in my mind. And there he was with the biggest, widest, warmest, most welcoming smile. It was his smile, the smile of a father, that won my young heart.

The Smile of the Father

A father's smile is a precious gift to a child. It conveys a very important message. First and foremost, it says, "I see you. You have my attention." *Attention is the most valued, expensive, treasured, and sought-after commodity in the universe.* And the heart of a child desperately desires to receive that paternal attention and with it their father's acceptance, affection, affirmation, and approval. What's so great about a father's smile is it can communicate all those things and all at once.

When I think of the smile of God our Father, I think of Jesus. *Jesus perfectly demonstrated the love of the Father to the world when He gave His life on the cross and made possible our redemption.* As we receive the gift of salvation, of life eternal, we experience the light of the countenance of the Father on our lives. That light, that smile, brings to us all the acceptance, affection, attention, and approval we could ever want. Since Jesus "is the image of the invisible God, the firstborn of all creation,"[1] and it's in Jesus that "the whole fullness of deity dwells bodily,"[2] *Jesus is not only the smile of God the Father, but Jesus is the perfect reflection—the perfect image or revelation—of God.* And the greatest revelation of God that Jesus gave to His disciples and us in His teaching and earthly ministry is the revelation of God as our Father.

God is not simply our Creator. He's not the clock-maker god, a distant or absent deity. *Jesus revealed God as the ultimate, perfect, consistent, emotionally available, protective, and redeeming Father.* Jesus was the perfect revelation of the Father, coming to Earth as Immanuel, to be God with us, and providing for us a way to personally come to the Father. He taught us the perfect invocation, how to pray by entreating our Father. And He also modeled for us the prototype of a child relating to the Father.

The Perfect Revelation

Any revelation of the Father starts with Jesus. Though Jesus came to reveal to us the very character and nature of God, as the Son, He is distinct from the Father. We spoke about the Trinity in the first chapter, identifying the three Persons of the Trinity—Father, Son, and Holy Spirit. These three Persons are One in essence, sharing one divine nature, yet distinct in personality. Only through Jesus can we come into a relationship with God as our Father. So, when we want to know who God the Father is, rather than looking at inconsistent and imperfect earthly examples of fathers, we should look to Jesus and all that Jesus revealed to us about the Father.

If the greatest revelation that Jesus gave to us is a reflection or an understanding of the Father, and if it's Jesus's most important revelation, that means it's crucial that we know God as Father. Knowing Him as Father is not a secondary issue, then.

In John 14, Jesus Himself had something to say about His identity and relationship with the Father. In the Upper Room in Jerusalem, the evening before His death, Jesus offered comfort to the disciples gathered with Him as He knew they would be facing His impending departure. He didn't want them anxious or afraid. He wanted them to believe in God, to believe in Him. He wanted to assure them of two things: (1) He was going to prepare a place for them, and (2) He would come again and take them to Himself.[3] And as a way to help them feel quite sure of all He had told them only moments before, as a type of guarantee that it all would be okay because they knew what He was talking about, Jesus said this, "And you know the way to where I am going."[4]

There was a problem, however. The disciples didn't know where He was going. They, as often was the case, were struggling to put together everything He had been telling them. They weren't getting it, any of it. One disciple, the one generations have dubbed "doubting Thomas," stuck his neck out there and said, "Lord, we do not know where you are going. How can we know the way?"[5]

To that, Jesus replied:

I am the way, and the truth, and the life. No one comes to the Father except through me. If you had known me, you would have known my Father also. From now on you do know him and have seen him.

— John 14:6–7

Next, Philip got brave and said in response, "Lord, show us the Father, and it is enough for us."[6] In a way, he was acknowledging that they didn't know the Father, that Jesus needed to show them the Father.

It must have really surprised them all when Jesus asked in response, "Have I been with you so long, and you still do not know me, Philip?" Thankfully, He went on to explain:

> Whoever has seen me has seen the Father. How can you say, "Show us the Father"? Do you not believe that I am in the Father and the Father is in me? The words that I say to you I do not speak on my own authority, but the Father who dwells in me does his works. Believe me that I am in the Father and the Father is in me, or else believe on account of the works themselves.
>
> — John 14:9–11

Although Jesus as the Son of God is a distinct Member of the Godhead, He responded to Philip, identifying Himself as the perfect revelation of the Father, that He was in the Father and the Father was in Him—that Father and Son were One. John Piper explained it this way, "The emphasis of verses 7–11 is crystal clear. Six times Jesus says virtually the same thing, that he and the Father are so profoundly one, that his presence is the presence of God the Father."[7] This truth of Jesus's being the perfect revelation of the Father is further established in Hebrews 1:1–3, where the writer explained:

> Long ago, at many times and in many ways, God spoke to our fathers by the prophets, but in these last days he has spoken to us by his Son, whom he appointed the heir of all things, through whom also he created the world. He is the

radiance of the glory of God and the exact imprint of his nature, and he upholds the universe by the word of his power.

The prophets proclaimed the Word of God. They spoke about God and spoke on His behalf. But then God sent His Son, Jesus, "who is Himself the Revelation, the Revealer, and the Revealed."[8] In other words, He is the One who reveals the Father to us. This is why Jesus said *He is the way to the Father, He is the truth of the Father, and He is the giver of life from the Father.* It's all through Jesus. And that's why Jesus could say, if we have seen Him, then we have seen the Father. If we know Jesus, then we know the Father.

The Perfect Invocation

Jesus said that He came to glorify the Father.[9] He came to show us the Father. Jesus came as the way, the truth, and the life so that we could connect with the heart of the Father and know Him. *There are certain things that are broken in our human condition that God will heal and make whole through a revelation of who He is as our Father.* That's why when Jesus taught us to pray, He said to use the two most revolutionary words, "Our Father."

Right in the middle of Jesus's famed Sermon on the Mount, Jesus taught His followers how to pray. Between the Beatitudes and His "do not worry" admonition, Jesus warned His disciples against the attention-seeking, public prayers of the hypocrites and countered it with these words: "But you, when you pray, go into your room, and when you have shut your door, pray to your Father who is in the secret place; and your Father who sees in secret will reward you openly."[10]

Jesus also warned His listeners against praying like another group of people. This time it was the Gentiles and their long, repetitious prayers. Instead of praying like the Gentiles, Jesus taught His disciples to pray what we call today "The Lord's Prayer":

> *Our Father in heaven,*
> *Hallowed be Your name.*
> *Your kingdom come.*
> *Your will be done*
> *On earth as it is in heaven.*
> *Give us this day our daily bread.*
> *And forgive us our debts,*
> *As we forgive our debtors.*
> *And do not lead us into temptation,*
> *But deliver us from the evil one.*
> *For Yours is the kingdom and the power*
> *And the glory forever. Amen.*

> — Matthew 6:9–13 NKJV

With these two words, "Our Father," Jesus ushered in a prayer revolution. Although prior generations of Jewish people had a general understanding of God as their Father, their invocations to Him more typically addressed Him as God, Yahweh, Creator, King of the universe, or the One—the Source from whom all life and blessing flowed. When Jesus taught His disciples to begin their prayers with "Our Father," He was redefining how His followers should approach and relate to God.[11] This was unprecedented, historic, revolutionary. *It would reach beyond prayer models and become a revelation of the relationship that is the natural habitat of effective prayer.*

In essence, Jesus was telling us that the starting point of prayer is realizing the relationship we have with the One to whom we're praying. We begin by recognizing who God is to us and who we are to Him. God is our Father. As our Father, He feeds us, teaches us, leads us, protects us, loves us, talks to us, and hears us. We have been intimately and lovingly created by our Father to know Him, to be known by Him, to be cared for by Him, and to walk and talk with Him in intimate fellowship and communion. Jesus was demonstrating for us what prayer should be about. It's about relationship. It's about submitting our lives to our Father, acknowledging our needs of provision, forgiveness, and deliverance, and asking Him to change things in this world so that they line up with the way He has purposed them in heaven.

I love what Rabbi Jason Sobel wrote about the Lord's Prayer. He said:

[Jesus] reminds us that we're not part of an organization—we're members of a family. We don't pray to a remote, aloof life force; we communicate with our Abba [Father] in complete dependence and trust. Ours is a faith meant to be personally experienced, not merely intellectually acknowledged.[12]

It's all about approaching the Father in prayer the way Jesus taught us. The way we approach Him is through Jesus, the perfect revelation of the Father, as the children of the Father.

The Perfect Prototype

Not only is Jesus the perfect revelation of the Father, but Jesus serves as the perfect Prototype for us of what it looks like to relate as sons and daughters to God our Father. In all four Gospels, Jesus demonstrated how to do everyday life and ministry with God as our Father. In John 5:19, when the Jews and religious leaders were asking Jesus why He had healed a man on the Sabbath, Jesus said, "Truly, truly, I say to you, the Son can do nothing of his own accord, but only what he sees the Father doing. For whatever the Father does, that the Son does likewise." Jesus only said and did what He saw the Father say and do. This is how we should live life in relation to the Father.

Jesus was divine, but we don't look at His life or ministry and say, "That's unattainable." We look at it as the pattern that we're supposed to follow because *Jesus humbled Himself and became like us so that we could humble ourselves and become like Him.*[13] That's the pattern. We're not supposed to live according to the pattern of the world that leads us in the course of this world, following the desires of our flesh. You and I were called to live according to the pattern of Jesus in perfect dependence on and obedience to the Father. This is what will produce an overflow of supernatural results like the overflow manifested in the life and earthly ministry of Jesus. That overflow in Jesus's life and ministry was a product of His intimacy with the Father.

Luke 5:16 tells us that, very often, Jesus would withdraw to a desolate place and pray. We see this in the other Gospels as well. When confronted with crowds of people, Jesus would withdraw and pray to the Father. Why? Because *Jesus's affirmation and His identity were not found in the crowd. They were found in the secret place with His Father.* Jesus only needed one Voice to tell Him who He was. Jesus was unaffected by the other voices because He was completely dependent on the Father. He wasn't dependent, however, out of some legal obligation. No, it was because He wanted to fellowship with His Father, it was because there He found direction, it was because there He experienced intimacy with the Father, and it was because there He received from His Father everything He needed to be obedient and fruitful.

Jesus was the perfect Son in perfect submission to the Father, yielding to the agenda and process of the Father. We want to follow in the footsteps of our Elder Brother Jesus.[14] Jesus partnered with the Father, modeling for us how we, too, should partner with the Father. Jesus's being a prototype of a son in relationship to the Father, if we'll have eyes to see it, can actually unwind a lot of the dysfunction and brokenness and barriers between us and God that have become established in our relationship with Him.

Prayer

Our Father, thank You for loving us. Thank You for sending us Your Son, Jesus, to reveal Yourself to us through Him. We want to grow in our understanding and knowledge of You as our Father. Help us to continue to see more of who You are in the perfect revelation of Your Son.

Jesus, thank You for being the way and the truth and the life, giving Your life and making it possible for us to come into relationship with the Father. We want to continue to honor the Father by following Your example and teaching.

Holy Spirit, continue to teach our hearts how to say, "Abba, Father," and to see our everyday lives as opportunities to know the Father more.

Reflection

1. What do you think about the metaphor of Jesus being the smile of the Father?

2. Reflecting on your prayer life, do you sometimes approach God like a distant authority figure rather than communicating with Him as your Heavenly Father? What from this chapter may help you approach God differently?

3. How is your current relationship with the Father like Jesus's relationship with the Father? How is it different?

4. Where do you most often seek affirmation? How can you cultivate the same "secret place" dependence Jesus modeled for us?

Chapter 3
Returning to the Father

My dad ran away. That's what he did. His abandoning me and my mom wasn't the first time he had left his home. He had left his childhood home a few years earlier at fifteen years of age. "Mick the Trick" was his nickname, and it adequately described him in the same way Jacob's name defined him. Dad had rebelled against the strict version of the Christian faith exercised in his parents' home. He had become rapt in sex, drugs, rock 'n' roll, and baseball. And in the hey-day of the hedonistic late 1960s and early 1970s, Mickey had left what should have been the safety of his home, taking with him the luggage of emotional pain from a childhood marked by excessive punishment from his father and the dark secrets of abuse from others. His introduction to sex and drug use at a very young age had ignited the fire of rebellion inside him, putting him in red-hot conflict with his family.

Dad's dream since just about the time he could talk had been to be a major league baseball player. Though his relationship with his own father was strained and emotionally distant, they always had seemed to connect around baseball. It had helped that Dad was an exceptional talent, a prospect pitcher with potentially a bright future before him.

About the time the doors of opportunity were opening for Dad to play in an entry-level minor league, two things occurred that brought his dream crashing down. First, his shoulder experienced the kind of pain and strain that indicated a torn rotator cuff, which was considered career-ending at that time. The second thing that happened to him was more personal to me. I was born. With that came the responsibility of providing for my mom and me. Dad was beginning to realize he would never make the major leagues. To medicate the pain of that and the overwhelm of taking care of a small family, he turned more fully to drugs, including heroine. Soon, he found himself living in a parallel universe of addiction.

This addiction was what compounded the difficulties he and my mother were already having in their marriage. My mom had found Jesus in the church services that my grandparents had invited her to. She had discovered the love of God and hoped He would save her marriage and change Mickey's heart. Night after night, however, my dad had come home late, high, and broke, having spent his paycheck on drugs. Of course, that didn't fly with my mother who had confronted him repeatedly. It was after too many fights and a moment in which Dad's anger was taken out on me, his nine-month-old son, that he decided to leave.

From there, my father moved in and out of my life. When he was present, he introduced me to things that a father *is supposed to* protect his son from, things like pornography, marijuana, and excessive alcohol use. He gave me a long leash to experiment with all that the world had to offer, acting more like a permissive elder brother to me. Although I would never use marijuana or drink alcohol, my exposure to pornography was unavoidable. My bedroom at his apartment was filled with magazines featuring scenes and images that drowned my innocence and awakened something impure inside my young heart.

Trying somehow to sort out his life, Dad started seeking some type of spirituality, picking, choosing, and intermixing New Age philosophies with Eastern mysticism, all on a self-styled spiritual journey of exploration. Much like the Luke 15 prodigal in Jesus's parable, it would take losing almost everything—in his case, a business and three marriages—before he came "home" to the Father and found his place in the family of God. He spent the last fifteen years of his life growing in his faith, wrestling free from his past, and serving others around him in a profound way. I'll forever be grateful to have witnessed his transformation and see the man God always wanted him to be.

The Lost Are Found

It was near the end of Jesus's ministry. He had been gathering large crowds of people wherever He went. This day was no different, only the Scripture tells us specifically who was among the crowd: tax collectors, sinners, scribes, and Pharisees.[1] The latter two were complaining about how Jesus received sinners and even ate with them. In response to this, we read that Jesus told them the parable of the man who lost one of a hundred sheep, leaving the ninety-nine to find the stray.[2] When he found the lost sheep, Jesus pointed out that the man invited all his friends and neighbors to celebrate.[3]

Then, Jesus told the crowd about the woman with ten silver coins who lost one. She swept her house clean and diligently sought the lost coin until she found it.[4] Once she found it, Jesus revealed that the woman with the lost coin did the same as the man who had found his lost sheep. She called her friends and neighbors together, asking them to rejoice with her.[5] And Jesus ended both parables by underscoring that there is great joy in heaven when one lost sinner repents.[6]

We might think that, surely, the hearers of these two parables would have gotten the message the first or, at least, the second time. *Jesus was responding to the judgmental, self-righteous scribes and Pharisees, showing how actively and lovingly God pursues the sinner, the lost individual, and how His love goes out to that one and celebrates when he or she repents and returns to Him.* But Jesus knew they needed to hear yet another parable, one in which the scribes and Pharisees as well as the sinners and tax collectors could see or find themselves within its storyline. So, He proceeded to tell them another parable, the one commonly known as the *parable of the prodigal son.*

The parable of the prodigal son is considered by many to be the greatest parable that Jesus ever taught. Why? Because it conveys the complexity of our relationship with our Heavenly Father and His deep, burning love for us. It's a revelation of the Father heart of God toward us in our lostness, toward us who have wandered far away from Him, as well as toward those elder brothers who are more like the scribes and Pharisees.

The Story of Two Sons and Their Father

Jesus began to tell the parable of the prodigal son to the crowd around Him. At the beginning, He let the crowd know the story was about two sons and their father. He said:

There was a man who had two sons. And the younger of them said to his father, "Father, give me the share of property that is coming to me." And he divided his property between them. Not many days later the younger son gathered all he had and took a journey into a far country, and there he squandered his property in reckless living.

— Luke 15:11–13

As if his blowing all his inheritance wasn't bad enough, Jesus then told His hearers that the country experienced "a severe famine," which caused the young man "to be in need."[7] In his desperate condition, he "hired himself out to one of the citizens of that country, who sent him into his fields to feed pigs." Going from bad to worse, the young man grew so hungry that he longed "to be fed with the pods that the pigs ate."[8] It was at this point that the young man "came to himself" and said,

How many of my father's hired servants have more than enough bread, but I perish here with hunger! I will arise and go to my father, and I will say to him, "Father, I have sinned against heaven and before you. I am no longer worthy to be called your son. Treat me as one of your hired servants."

— Luke 15:17–19

Jesus continued the story, sharing that the young man left to return to his father's house, rehearsing along the way what he would say to his father once he arrived back home. How would he explain that which was unexplainable? How could he justify how low he had gotten and how easily he had sold his own soul? What Jesus described next must have been evocative to those listening to Him. For while the son was yet a distance away, the father saw him, "felt compassion" for him, "and ran and embraced him and kissed him."[9] Unthinkable. His was a scandalous response to the filth and shame walking toward him.

This is a story of a father who never gave up hope. It's a story of a father who, although he had been completely dishonored and abandoned, never stopped loving his son. He never stopped looking on the horizon for his son to come home. Much like the man with the lost sheep and the woman with the lost coin, the father wanted what had been lost to him to be found, to return to him.

Amazingly, the father wasn't in the living room with his arms folded. He had not changed the locks. He had not made rash statements like, "Leave and you will never be welcomed back. If you take your inheritance today, know that you are dead to me! You're no longer my son." No, it had been the son who had disowned and dishonored his dad.

When the young man had the chance, however, he confessed his sin "against heaven and before" his father, acknowledging he was "no longer worthy to be called" his father's son.[10] And then something incredible happened. The father told his servants,

Bring quickly the best robe, and put it on him, and put a ring on his hand, and shoes on his feet. And bring the fattened calf and kill it, and let us eat and celebrate. For this my son was dead, and is alive again; he was lost, and is found.

— Luke 15:22–24

When Jesus taught this parable, He was teaching something that was and is very difficult for the human heart in its selfishness and sinfulness to understand, which is the fatherly heart and everlasting love that God has for us. This was quite a departure from what the religious of that day thought about God. To the scribe and Pharisee, religion was easy to understand. "Give us a checklist of things we need to do to be right, and we'll do them, and then we'll get God's approval." But this love—the kind shown by the father in the parable, who gave his son not only his inheritance but anything he needed when the son returned broke and broken, even celebrating him with a feast—was extravagant, extraordinary, utterly unheard of. In the face of the religious arrogance, the thought that they could do anything of themselves which would please God, Jesus's teaching about the unconditional love of the Father was a slap across their independent and rebellious faces.

The son's willingness to return as a servant, believing that was all he was worthy of, would have seemed entirely logical to those hearing the parable. Yet when the father saw his son, the father didn't exact retribution or payback from the young man. He didn't subjugate the young man to indenture through servanthood or slavery, which the younger son appeared to expect. Instead, the father *fully* restored the relationship with his son. He put a ring on his son's finger. A signet ring was like the father's credit card in that the son could access any resources of his father's with the stamp of that ring. Then, the father put a robe on his returned son. The garments of the prodigal son bearing the marks and stains of the pigpen, of immoral living, were removed, and the robe of righteousness or sonship was placed on him. New shoes were put on his feet that changed the way he walked. He no longer bore the cuts and scars and filth and dirt of his own pursuit or wanderings. His journey was finally covered by the grace and the goodness of his father. And as if that weren't enough, the father threw a party to welcome his once lost son home. Seems like a great place to end this story, but the story wasn't over yet. There was another son in the story—the elder brother who stayed with the father and worked the family business.

We must remember Jesus was telling a story about a family, about a father and his two sons. There was brokenness in this family, and it wasn't a matter of one broken relationship between the father and the younger son. All the relationships among the three were fractured in some way. Each son's relationship with the father was and so was the relationship between the brothers themselves. In fact, the elder brother was out working in the fields when his kid brother had returned home. Unbeknown to the elder brother, the festivities had already started when he began his return to the family home from the fields. Jesus explained that the elder brother heard the music as he approached the house, provoking him to ask a servant what all the commotion was about. After the elder brother heard the explanation given by the servant —that his brother had come home and the father had "killed the fattened calf" and "received" his brother—the elder brother was angry and refused to go into the celebration and welcome his brother back home.[11] He wasn't about to welcome his kid brother back into the family after all the younger brother had done. *If the younger brother was the rebel, the elder brother was the one who was religious, the one who had been attempting to gain right standing with the father by his best behavior.*

According to the parable, the father then came out to the elder son and "entreated him" to come into the party, but the elder brother wasn't interested.[12] He told his dad:

Look, these many years I have served you, and I never disobeyed your command, yet you never gave me a young goat, that I might celebrate with my friends. But when this son of yours came, who has devoured your property with prostitutes, you killed the fattened calf for him!

— Luke 15:29–30

Notice the separation the elder brother made by saying, "this son of yours." He was done with how his brother's decisions had hurt the family, and to top it all off, the father was doing something for his no-good brother that the father had never done for him, the son who had stayed and worked in the family business.

The father appealed once more to his elder son, saying, "Son, you are always with me, and all that is mine is yours. It was fitting to celebrate and be glad, for this your brother was dead, and is alive; he was lost, and is found."[13] And that's the end of the parable. Full stop.

What a way to end the story, leaving it unresolved. It's not how most of us like stories to end. We like our stories all stitched up, clean, neat, and tidy. Father and younger son's relationship all redeemed and restored. Father and elder son's relationship all healed and whole. Elder brother and younger brother's relationship all mended and enduring to at least middle age. But Jesus didn't do that for the crowd or for us. He left the story a little incomplete for our taste, yet perfectly impactful in that leaving the story unresolved made hearers engage more with the story and the possible outcomes. Redemption, restoration, healing, and right relationship remained possible but definitely not guaranteed. In fact, you and I might wager that the elder brother, like the Pharisees, would be more apt to stay the course in rejecting the brother and acting self-righteous and outraged toward the father. Jesus left the story in the unresolved tension because the story belongs to us all. The question of how we will respond to the radical love of God is yet to be determined by each of us.

Timothy Keller in his book *The Prodigal God* said the hearts of both sons were "alienated from the father's heart; both were lost sons."[14] The younger went and sowed his wild seeds, while the eldest stayed but allowed the seeds of bitterness and resentment to grow into full-grown weeds of the same. When describing Jesus's message, Keller said this:

Neither son loved the father for himself. They both were using the father for himself. They both were using the father for their own self-centered ends rather than loving, enjoying, and serving him for his own sake. This means that you can rebel against God and be alienated from him either by breaking his rules *or* by keeping all of them diligently.

It's a shocking message: Careful obedience to God's law may serve as a strategy for rebelling against God.[15]

See, the elder brother was keeping all the rules, but it wasn't out of love. I can imagine him thinking, *I'm going to please my dad. He will affirm me, and someday, he'll give me everything he has. He won't deny me anything because I've worked, I've slaved for it.* Obviously, when he saw the grace his father showed his younger brother, the one who had taken his inheritance and spent it on riotous living, the elder brother was offended as he evaluated who was deserving of the grace, the favor, of the father. The elder brother judged based on who performed the best. And, if that had been the criterion, the elder brother would have been the winner, hands down. But the father never saw the sons that way. *The father saw the sons through his loving fatherly heart. He loved them because they were his sons.* He was not only willing to redeem and restore them to himself and his family, but also he wanted to reconcile with them and have them reconciled to *each other.*

Fatherlessness is not always manifested by us rejecting God and going and running off into the world as sinners, partying and doing whatever we want and someday saying, "I'm so sorry, God. Forgive me. Restore me," and then, in mercy, we receive that. Sometimes, our fatherlessness is dressed up in religion, a relationship with God that's based on our performance without a true heart connection with God as our Father. God wants our hearts. He wants a relationship with you and me. *God wants to heal the wounds and the scars of fatherlessness manifested as rebellion as well as fatherlessness disguised by religion.*

Can I tell you that it takes God to love God? First John 4:19 explains, "We love because he first loved us." We can only love Him because we have been the recipients of His love. What's more, only those who have the Spirit of Christ and are led by the Spirit of God are children of God.[16] We need the help of the Holy Spirit, of God, not only to learn to know who God the Father is, but to learn to love God as Father. I'll say it again: It takes God to love God. And remember Galatians 4:6, where the apostle Paul wrote that because we're God's children, "God has sent the Spirit of his Son into our hearts, crying, 'Abba! Father!' So you are no longer a slave." We're children and "heirs through God" as verse 7 states.

Like in the parable, when we come to God, He puts the ring on us, He puts the robe on us, He puts the sandals on us, and He throws the feast. This is how the Father welcomes us into His family and shows us what it means to be a son or a daughter who is loved by Him solely because we're His kids! Whether we've grabbed our inheritance and blown it on all the wrong stuff or stayed in His house yet remained distant and dedicated to working hard for His acceptance and love that were already available to us for free, it's time to return to the Father. It's time to come home and let Him lavish on us the glory and splendor of His fatherly love.

Prayer

Father, we still at times struggle to believe in the depth of Your grace and love. Even after wasting the gifts You've given us, even turning our backs on You and chasing after everything else, You remain at the end of the road—watching, waiting, and longing for us to come home.

Lord, even in our pride, when we have insisted on trying to fix ourselves, following every rule, and earning Your love, You still whisper the same truth, that You've always loved us. It has never been about perfection or performance. It's always been about our hearts.

Thank You, Holy Spirit, for bringing us to our senses. That while we have wallowed in the pigpen of our own insecurities and sin, You've caused us to realize it's not what we truly want. Thank You for awakening us to our need of the love of the Father and helping us to return to Him. Thank You, Jesus, for making a way for us to come home. Thank You, Father, for putting on us a robe of a new nature, giving us shoes to change the way we walk, and throwing us a feast, welcoming us back into Your house and into Your family.

Reflection

1. How does the story of Mickey Cummings mirror the prodigal son's journey of rebellion, brokenness, and eventual return? Is there anything in your story that parallels the parable or Mickey's story?

2. In what ways do both sons in Jesus's parable represent different forms of separation from the Father? How might either of these attitudes show up in your own relationship with God?

3. What does this story reveal about the heart of God the Father toward those who feel unworthy or distant from Him?

4. How does Mickey's story of redemption and transformation encourage you to believe that no one is too far gone for the Father's love, redemption, and restoration?

5. How does the father's response in Luke 15 challenge your view of forgiveness and unconditional love as these relate to God the Father?

Chapter 4
Belonging to the Father

Mom and Dad divorced. I continued to live with Mom, and she worked at a department store and served as a waitress at a local diner to make sure we had a roof over our heads and food on our table. After some time, she met a man at her work whose name was Bob and decided it was time to bring him home to meet me, her then six-year-old son.

You definitely could say their relationship was a whirlwind romance in that they were married within six weeks of their first date, barely giving me enough time to get comfortable with my mom having a suitor, let alone her having a husband who wasn't my dad. All I could tell at my young age was my mom was the happiest I had seen her in quite some time, and she was spending all her time with Bob. Like any newlyweds, they were focused on each other and making a life together.

The early years of this new family I found myself in were promising but also confusing. After only a year, we moved across the state to Grand Rapids for Bob's new job. Moving away from all that was familiar, I had to figure out how to navigate living in a new neighborhood, attending a new school, making new friends, and confronting the complicated reality of having two very different dads. Kids are highly adaptive, and I did the best I could; however, the internal pain and fear of what this new reality meant for me were deeply felt. I spent long hours trying to untangle the knot of confusion and sense of loss that I didn't have words for or could articulate. I just felt lost.

In the years to come, as I grew into adolescence, more change came to my family. I was nine when my mom told me she was pregnant. I was a bit excited to think I was going to have a sibling. I would no longer be alone. I'd have someone, a brother or a sister, to do life with. Maybe I would finally feel like I belonged and knew who I really was. When my little brother was born, I was totally enthralled with him, and like most big brothers, I was looking forward to all the fun things we could do together. I drew pictures of him and called him "bright eyes" because he had such big brown eyes.

A few years later, another little brother came on the scene as I was becoming a teenager and starting to be more independent. Then it hit me with a sting I wasn't ready for: The brother I'd grown up with was actually my half-brother, and this new baby would be, too—yet the two of them would share something I never fully had with either of them. They would be full-blooded brothers, inheriting DNA from the same mother and father. And they would share the same last name, a name I didn't have. I wondered then what that would mean for me and how it would affect my relationships with both brothers, my stepfather, and my mother. Between my growing independence and this new brother's arrival, I was feeling more and more like an outsider, an add-on to someone else's family. Though I didn't need any more proof to support that feeling, something else happened that became the quintessential evidence of my being the odd kid out.

One day, I overheard my mom and stepdad arguing. They didn't know I heard them, though. I remember Mom was apologizing to Bob for something. I couldn't quite make out part of what she had said, but what I did hear cut me deeply. She said something about Bob "taking her with all of her mistakes and past baggage" when he had married her. I immediately thought, *That's me. I'm one of her mistakes. They're talking about me.* In my mind, I was the added baggage, and I felt like it. From that moment on, I knew I didn't fit into the family. Whether that is what my mom meant, I don't know, but what is certain is that I believed it. And what I perceived myself to be—a mistake or past baggage—cut me deeply and left me with a gaping gash in my soul.

I am grateful, however, for the home I grew up in and the roles my mother and my stepdad played in my life. My mom loved and cared for me as her firstborn, and my stepdad taught me discipline and integrity. He provided for Mom and me in a way that so many mothers and their children never experience. Bob was a good father to me, but the pain point was that he loved his two biological sons differently than he loved me. I was the stepson. I have to believe that being a stepparent is one of the most difficult jobs on the planet. To find a way to love another man's son is a tall task. Bob made a valiant attempt at it, but at the end of the day, blood is irreplaceable. My mother repeated again and again that they loved me the same as my little brothers, but deep down I knew those words described the world they wished for—not the one I had experienced.

My high school years were both beautiful and challenging. I encountered the Lord at age twelve. But there were also hard years because I felt like an outsider in our home. I kept myself busy with sports, friends, and youth group. As I got older, the tension between my parents and me only grew. I know today that much of that conflict was my fault because of my own stubbornness and the walls I had erected. But it was also very clear to me that they were looking forward to the day I moved out and they could have their "family" without me.

Within a few years, it was time for me to start college. Mom and Bob informed me that they preferred for me to live in the college dorm even though the school was a mile and a half away from home. I wasn't completely surprised by their request. It only underscored the disconnect I felt from them and my brothers. The hope of the little six-year-old boy ever feeling like he had a true place in his family, like he belonged, never became a reality. It was the goodness of God that saved me and called me in my youth, solidifying in my heart that, even if I didn't see the fulness of what it was like to live in a fully formed human family, God Himself was indeed my Father. The Church was where I felt at home, and the process of God restoring the broken image of my identity as a son was already underway.

Our Greatest Need

The greatest need in the human heart is to be loved and to belong. In 1943, Abraham Maslow wrote a paper titled, "A Theory of Human Motivation," which identified five basic sets of needs. It has since become known as "Maslow's Hierarchy of Needs."[1] Maslow's Hierarchy is often shown as a pyramid. At its base are the most basic physiological needs—air, food, water, and shelter. At the top is self-actualization, the need for personal growth and the pursuit of one's full potential. In the middle lies the essential human need for love and belonging. It occupies the third level, following physiological and safety needs, and preceding the fourth and fifth levels of esteem and self-actualization.[2] Another way to say this is the need to belong is the first most important need after our physiological and safety needs have been met. *Our primary need of belonging translates into our need to be a part of something that shapes and affirms our identity.* We need to receive the love of family and friends, to have the sense of connection and acceptance from the same.

Through the years, psychologists have researched and written about *belongingness.* They have found that we have a need, not merely a desire, to belong, and the threat of feeling excluded or of not belonging is the "primal ache" inside the human soul.[3]

The need to belong affects much of our lives, many of the decisions we make, and much of the way we present ourselves to the world. In studying what happens when we feel lonely or sense we don't belong, some researchers have identified three "dimensions of loneliness," which basically point to the kind of relationships we're not experiencing: emotional (intimate) loneliness, relational (social) loneliness, and collective (community) loneliness.[4] *Loneliness is a psychological way of describing that ache, that dull sense and longing we have to be known as we really are and to be loved and accepted just the same.*

There's so much fragmentation in our society, much from the fatherlessness we discussed in chapter one. And that primal ache has grown into something that American society as a whole is venting. We're all trying to find where we fit, where life makes sense, and where we understand that we matter. We're spiritual wanderers, moving through life in search of a home, a place where we will be loved and accepted for who we really are.

Born into the dysfunctional family called *the family of Adam,* we've been plagued by rebellion and sin. And that universal family has been negatively impacted by our individual dysfunctions as well. *Should we decide to be transparent about ourselves, we would acknowledge that part of the problem with our not possessing a true sense of belonging in our hearts is due to our own betrayal and rejection of others, especially our rejection of God, His perfect love, and His plans for us.*

Spiritually speaking, we all have trauma and trust issues as a result. And we have some attachment disorders, too. We try to protect ourselves in our relationships, even in our relationships with God. But the real problem has never been about God being untrustworthy or about God rejecting us. Time and again, we've pushed God away—God who is the one place where we can finally be our true selves and the one place where we are loved without condition.

You see, our existence and mattering don't come into clarity by belonging in just any people or community group. Our mattering manifests more unmistakably in relationship when we're in right relationship with the very One we've rejected. You may struggle with what I just said, but let's face it, we've been born into a world that has endeavored to push God away from the very beginning. Whether we realize it our not, we have been conditioned in our dysfunction to do the same.

For many years, I thought, *If I really give my life to God full throttle, He's going to make me unhappy.* I thought that He would take away the things that I had worked so hard to track down, the things I thought brought me happiness. And I was convinced He would judge me for the things I used to anesthetize the pain of the primal ache and the longing in my heart. I figured He would somehow force me into doing some things I didn't want to do, was uncomfortable doing, or would be miserable doing. But that simply wasn't true. Besides, all the stuff I thought would dull the ache or remove the ache were very limited in their ability to do so. These things didn't come through for me. At their very best, they afforded me a temporary respite from the loneliness of not having found home.

In the end, the one place where I was most safe, where I was most loved, and where I could become the most like I always knew I was created to be was in the Presence of my Heavenly Father. See, the reality is we're all born far away from home, but then one day, we wake up and say like the prodigal son, "I don't like it here in the pigpen. I want to go home. I'll return to my Father." The pigpen we wake up in may look different for each of us, but make no mistake about it, you and I were not created to live there. Jesus made a way for us to come home to the Father.

Waking Up

In the moment that we finally wake up in a far-off land and feel as if we've had our fill of unfulfilled pursuits, that's when we realize we don't have any more emotional energy, any more creative ideas, any more food. It's then we come to ourselves, realizing we're still in need and no human being or material possession or drug can ever fully satisfy the longing of our hearts to belong. It's in this moment that we come to our senses.

There's a moment, that's an awakening, where we find ourselves disillusioned with the pursuit of belonging in the things of the world, and we begin to find ourselves and recognize that we're in need of something that only God Himself can provide for us. Here's what

God does for us while we're waking up to the fact that we're at the dead end of ourselves:

> And you were dead in the trespasses and sins in which you once walked, following the course of this world, following the prince of the power of the air, the spirit that is now at work in the sons of disobedience [that's us]—among whom we all once lived in the passions of our flesh, carrying out the desires of the flesh and the mind, and were by nature children of wrath, like the rest of mankind. But God, being rich in mercy, because of the great love with which he loved us, even when were were dead in our trespasses, made us alive together with Christ—by grace you have been saved—and raised up with him and seated us with him in the heavenly places in Christ Jesus, so that in the coming ages he might show the immeasurable riches of his grace in kindness toward us in Christ Jesus. For by grace you have been saved through faith. And this is not your own doing; it is the gift of God, not a result of works, so that no one may boast.

> — Ephesians 2:1–9

These words the apostle Paul penned express the beautiful, wonderful, glorious gift of God to us. Think about it. Right when we were "carrying out the desires of our flesh" and wallowing in the muddy pigpen with nothing left—"dead in" our "trespasses and sins"—we were loved by God who is "rich in mercy." We had betrayed God, rebelled against Him, and resisted Him because we couldn't possibly fathom that He would have known what was best for us or that He wouldn't judge and condemn us. Theologically, you and I do deserve His judgment for what we have done. We deserve His judgment simply because we've been born into the human race, born into sin. In all justice, God could have looked at the race of Adam and said, "You know what? I'm washing My hands of you all. You've rejected Me. I'm done. I reject you now." But that's not what He did. Why? Because *God is not a God who runs away from us. God is a God who runs toward us.* He's a God who, according to the parable of the prodigal, looks for us, watches for us, longing for our return to Him, to where we belong.

Remember when Jesus said the father ran, embraced, and kissed his son? You see, the father would have had to pick up his gown and shown his feet in order to run to his son. In Middle Eastern culture, what the father did was undignified to do. The father's actions would have been seen as weakness to those watching him in the story and to those hearing the parable. I'm pretty sure the returning son didn't see his father's actions that way. He saw what his father was willing to do to have his son back. The father wasn't going to waste a moment waiting for the son's long walk of humiliation to be completed. He took off running as soon as the son came into sight, stumbling in his direction. Jesus was telling His listeners and us vicariously, like the father in the parable, God is not passively waiting for us to figure out how to get to Him. God knows the ache in the human heart. He sees our brokenness, loneliness, and pain, and He runs to us. There's nothing more powerful than to realize that God is not static. No, beloved, God the Father pursues us.

Think about all the broken perspectives that we have of who God is. How often do we project what we think of our earthly fathers on our Heavenly Father? As a result, some of us see God as cold and cruel, so we run from Him. We see God as angry and abusive, so we keep Him at an arm's length. Maybe we see God in our paradigm as absent and neglectful; therefore, we can't trust Him. These various perspectives keep us from turning to God. Yet God is committed to healing all the wrong perspectives and the broken places of detachment and self-protection that keep us from loving God and being loved by Him as Father. And when He helps us see Him as the God who runs toward and pursues us, we begin to understand that He is loving and present, that we don't have to convince Him to accept us, and that He has made a place for us in His house and at His table.

The reality is that Jesus doesn't simply walk with us by our side. Jesus sends His Holy Spirit inside us to heal our broken places, to tear down the false imaginations that have kept us as prisoners, and to rebuild a fortress of security in the Father's arms. This is what it means to be born again. This is what it means to come alive. Yes, we were dead. In our trespasses and in our spiritual deadness, we've rebelled against God and pursued reckless, prodigal living, trying to find a place to belong, something that satisfies, something that soothes the internal ache that says we're not sure we matter or belong. But Jesus, as our Elder Brother, has made a way to bring us into the household, the family of God, and then God puts His Spirit in us, that Spirit becomes the One who awakens the love of God in us and convinces us that we are children of God.

> For all who are led by the Spirit of God are sons of God. For you did not receive the spirit of slavery to fall back into fear, but you have received the Spirit of adoption as sons, by whom we cry, "Abba! Father!" The Spirit himself bears witness with our spirit that we are children of God.
>
> — Romans 8:14–16

The Holy Spirit is training us from the inside out to know God. And the very first thing, His primary occupation, the Holy Spirit in you, is to teach you how to say back to God, "Father!" The Holy Spirit in you is helping you to receive the love of the Heavenly Father. You see, when it's God's love that causes us to be loved and to belong, and we feel like we are loved and we belong, then what happens is it helps us to believe and to mature as sons and daughters of the living God, which is exactly what God has called us to do.

So, what do we do with this reality that God's pursuing us, that He loves us? For some of us, that's setting our sights on returning home. That's the first place, the first step. For all of us, it's coming to our senses, realizing God loves us personally, individually, and corporately. We realize we can come to Him, and we don't have to be afraid of Him. We recognize He alone has everything that we need to be healed and to belong. He can forgive our sins, yes, but He can also heal our hearts, convincing us that He loves us as our Father. But for some of us, we've already come home, yet we're still not convinced of these truths about the Father. We still have a little bit of an orphan attitude in our hearts toward the Lord, and it might be we simply need to say to God, "Father, it's not You. It's me. It's my pride that says, 'I think I'm still going to search out some other things. I think I can belong. I think I can find fulfillment and satisfaction in some other places. I'm going to check those out first.'" It means letting down our guard, rejecting the lies that we have believed, and experiencing the love of the Father with our hearts wide open.

Beloved, those other things we go after to find satisfaction serve as mirages, promising fulfillment but ultimately leading to the pig pen, to famine, and to us being in a place of need. For some of us, it's shame that says, "I don't know if I can really relate to

God. I don't know that He wants to be my Father, because I can't imagine He would want somebody like me. You don't know what I've done. You don't know what I've seen. You don't know how far my rebellion and my doubt, my pride, have gone, and I'm ashamed." We look down at the stains of shame and condemnation that cover our lives like those filthy garments of the prodigal son, asking ourselves, "How could He ever want me? I'm content to simply be a servant. I'll come to church. I'll make it into heaven, but, man, to really think that God wants to be a father to me, I doubt it."

Maybe the thing that's keeping you from fully coming home is guilt. "I'm still carrying some things, and I'm trying to get those things straightened out, trying to become the best version of myself. I'm feeling guilty that I've done it all wrong up until now. I've done too much. There's no way He'll accept me."

Or maybe it's fear. See, we're still waiting for God's judgments to come on us. It's like we're expecting Him to pull the rug out from under our feet or for Him not to show up when He said He was going to.

I want to say to you with all clarity and love that what fills the Father's heart for us is compassion. I'm so grateful for the mercies and the compassion of God. I'm so grateful that, when God sees me, He doesn't run away from me—He runs to me! And He doesn't do that for me alone. His eyes are filled with compassion for you. Can I promise you today that nothing you have ever done has caught God off guard? God isn't looking at you, thinking, *That's a new one. Wow, that's excessive! That's extreme. I don't know if I can forgive that. I'm not sure if I want them.* The truth is God desires you more than you know.

Paul wrote to the believers in Corinth about God welcoming them into His family. He said this while urging them to separate themselves from the world and its idolatry. He then used language that echoed God's promises in Isaiah 52:11 and 2 Samuel 7:14 for those who do. Paul asserted:

> What agreement has the temple of God with idols? For we are the temple of the living God; as God said, "I will make my dwelling among them and walk among them, and I will be their God, and they shall be my people. Therefore go out from their midst, and be separate from them, says the Lord, and touch no unclean thing; then I will welcome you, and I will be a father to you, and you shall be sons and daughters to me, says the Lord Almighty."

> — 2 Corinthians 6:16–18

Here's the master key to the Kingdom that opens the door to health and wholeness in life. It's understanding the revelation of God as our Father. Only in Him do we finally find our home and experience the acceptance, security, and even shared destiny within a family, the family of God. It's here that God makes His dwelling with us and He walks among us like He walked with Adam and Eve in the cool of the day.

Ephesians 2:13 says, "But now in Christ Jesus you who were once far off have been brought near by the blood of Christ." On your journey—looking for purpose, mattering, and belonging— you have now been brought near, not by your good works, but by the blood of Christ, for He Himself is your peace. Today is the day for you to stop running, leave your shame, guilt and pride by the wayside, and come home. God desires so much more for us than merely to believe in Him. He wants us to know Him as Father. He wants us to know that we belong in His family so that we know we matter and belong, so that we can become like Him.

Prayer

Father, thank You that You have welcomed us into Your family. Thank You for being my home, my place of belonging. We confess the primal ache that still rises within us when we allow shame, guilt, condemnation, or pride to convince us that we do not belong to You. Please forgive us and let Your love be shed abroad in hearts afresh today.

Jesus, thank You for being our Way, for bringing us near the Father through Your blood. Thank You for showing us the Father, for demonstrating to us His great love for us. Thank You for being our Elder Brother and interceding for us.

Holy Spirit, thank You for marking us as children of the Father, for serving as the guarantee of our salvation, and for not allowing anything to separate us from the Father's love in Christ Jesus.

Reflection

1. How does Lee's experience with his family shape his understanding of love and belonging? How do you think it may have influenced his view of God as Father?

2. In what ways have you experienced or witnessed the primal ache of not belonging in yourself or others, and how have you or they tried to fill it?

3. How does Maslow's idea that love and belonging are basic needs help you understand pain and longing you may have experienced in your life?

4. Which kind of loneliness (emotional, relational, or collective) do you relate to most? How might a deeper relationship with God the Father address that specific kind of loneliness?

Chapter 5
Adopted by the Father

How would you like to change your last name so that it's the same as ours? We'll all have the same last name, like a normal family," they said, trying to persuade me that a name change would make us one happy family. Mom and Bob had sat me down and asked me this question that I totally didn't expect, a question too big for an eight-year-old to process.

I am sure that they had no idea of how confusing or painful such a question would be for me. They had nothing but the best intentions in mind, but the sense of being put in a position to choose between my mom and this new family unit *and* my dad and grandparents was too much for my young heart to take. When I look back at that time, I don't think even a legal adoption itself would have made any difference in how I felt about belonging to my family. Maybe a legal document would have only reminded me of what I felt then—that I wasn't a real member of the family. In the end, it was a no-go because my grandparents stepped in and informed my mother that I was a Cummings and would always be a Cummings. And that was the end of the name change or pseudo-adoption talk. To this day, I am grateful that I kept my family name.

Sons and Daughters

In 2 Corinthians 5:17, Paul wrote, "Therefore, if anyone is in Christ, he is a new creation. The old has passed away; behold, the new has come." When we repent, acknowledge Jesus as Lord, and are born again by the Spirit of God, we are made new—completely new—in Christ. What Jesus accomplished on the cross for us removes our shame, restores the perfect image of God to us, makes us righteous, restores authority and dominion to us, and most of all, it connects us back to God. We no longer have to hide behind trees like Adam and Eve. We can draw near to our Father, being perfectly intimate and close with Him without shame, filters, or fig leaves.

The Holy Spirit comes into us when we open ourselves, when we believe the gospel, "For God so loved the world, that he gave his only Son, that whoever believes in him should not perish but have eternal life."[1] When we believe that, and we open up our hearts to that, God comes to us. He puts His Spirit within us as a down payment, a guarantee of our adoption and acceptance. And the very first thing the Holy Spirit does, His primary occupation in us, is to teach us how to communicate with the Father. Having received the "Spirit of adoption as sons," we cry, "Abba! Father!"[2]

The Holy Spirit is also the One who pours out the love of the Father in our hearts.[3] That's how the Holy Spirit heals our orphaned hearts. He allows us to be loved by God, to experience the Father's heart for us. You see, when God's Spirit causes us to be awash in the love of the Father, and when we experience that love and sense of belonging it generates, then what happens is it helps us to believe and to become sons and daughters of the living God, which is exactly what God calls us. Remember 1 John 3:1 declares, "See what kind of love the Father has given to us, that we should be called children of God; and so we are."

John 1:12–13 offers this insight about becoming the children of God. John said this about those who accept Christ Jesus:

> But to all who did receive him, who believed in his name, he gave the right to become children of God, who were born, not of blood nor of the will of the flesh nor of the will of man, but of God.

Exousia is the Greek word used and translated in the above verses as "the right to become." That word means right, privilege, power, or capacity. When we believe, then, we receive the right, the privilege, the power, or the capacity to become God's children. Who gives us this power? God does when we believe in His Son.

The apostle Paul wrote to the Ephesians, clarifying how it is that God gives us this power. It's through adoption. He explained:

> Blessed be the God and Father of our Lord Jesus Christ, who has blessed us in Christ with every spiritual blessing in the heavenly places, even as he chose us in him before the foundation of the world, that we should be holy and blameless before him. In love he predestined us for adoption to himself as sons through Jesus Christ, according to the purpose of his will.
>
> — Ephesians 1:3–6

God has purposes and plans designed for us from eternity past, as any parent has dreams in their heart for their future children. God the ultimate Father has prepared a purpose and a path for each of us even before we took our first breath. In His foreknowledge, for example, He has predestined us for adoption as His children. That means we no longer have to be slaves to fear, sin, guilt, and shame. We no longer have to live as orphans. Instead, we can live as sons and daughters adopted by the Father and welcomed into His family with the full rights and privileges as His children and heirs. Galatians 4:7 confirms this, saying, "So you are no longer a slave, but a son, and if a son, then an heir through God."

What the Father Provides

As sons and daughters, we have access to the things our Heavenly Father provides, things like love, salvation, eternal life, help, presence, and so much more. Thinking of our earthly fathers, there are typically five things we look to them to provide: life, shelter, protection, identity, and discipline. The good news is, whether we were given these by our earthly fathers or not, we are recipients of these five things now from God the Father.

God the Father gives us life. John 3:16 tells us He gives us eternal life through belief in His Son. John 10:10 says Jesus came to us to give us abundant life. Our biological parents both provided life and DNA; however, the majority of DNA that's passed on to a child is from the father. It's what we typically refer to as the seed from the father. Scripture tells us that God's seed abides in us and that we were born again of an "imperishable" seed, "through the living and abiding word of God."[4] What's so incredible about being adopted by God is that we can receive in our spiritual adoption something we can never receive in an earthly adoption. With an earthly adoption, we get a new name and the rights and privileges that come with it, but we can never receive the DNA of our adoptive parents here on earth. However, we can and do receive the spiritual DNA of our Father in heaven who has adopted us. As one writer has explained it:

> We begin to share the genetic encoding of God Himself as His Word is releasing it in us. Not only is His Word releasing it, but His Spirit is in us doing the same thing. So it's a combination of Word and Spirit.
>
> . . . So there is really a transformation of something within us. It isn't metaphorical. It isn't hypothetical, but it's actual. . . . The best analogy, the best terminology I could use is we receive of His genetic encoding—the genetic coding of our Savior Himself.[5]

The apostle Peter said it most simply when He said that sons and daughters of God "may become partakers of the divine nature."[6]

The second thing our Heavenly Father provides for us is shelter. We become a part of His household.[7] As a part of His household, He gives us sustenance, clothing, and stability. In Luke 12:22–28, Jesus admonished the disciples not to "be anxious" about their lives, about what they would eat or what they would wear. They didn't have to worry because, as Jesus said in verse 30, "Your Father knows that you need" these things. At another time, Jesus told the disciples He was going to His "Father's house," where He would "prepare a place for" them (and us).[8] God the Father is our Home. He is our Shelter. He is our Provider.[9]

Thirdly, our Father in heaven is our Defender and our Protector. Throughout Scripture, we see how God the Father has defended and protected His children. When we become a son or daughter of

His, He offers us that same protection. The writer of Hebrews said, "So we can confidently say, 'The Lord is my helper; I will not fear; what can man do to me?'"[10] Paul told believers in 2 Thessalonians 3:3 that the Lord will be faithful to guard them "against the evil one." The Lord is our defense. He will take care of us, His children.

The fourth thing our Father provides is our identity. This is what the Father spoke over Jesus when He was baptized by John the Baptist. Remember, the heavens opened up, and the Spirit descended "on him like a dove. And a voice came from heaven, 'You are my beloved Son; with you I am well pleased.'"[11] Do you know that, immediately after that moment, Jesus was driven into the wilderness by the Holy Spirit to be tempted by the devil? And the very first temptation that the devil came and gave to Jesus at His weakest moment, after having fasted for forty days and nights, was a challenge to Jesus's identity. The devil said to Him, "If you are the Son of God, command these stones to become loaves of bread."[12] The devil challenged Jesus's identity that the Father had spoken over Him right before Jesus went into the wilderness. The enemy, who is the liar, the father of lies, will always challenge your identity. This is his primary target because, if our sense of identity collapses, every other pillar of our confidence goes down with it. Identity is not some peripheral issue; it is a cornerstone of stability, and our Heavenly Father will always speak and affirm it. It's what a good father does. A father is supposed to cover his children, not just give them his name, but speak and help shape their identity.

Lastly, our Father provides direction. A father disciplines and brings course correction to his children so that, when they're young, they're able to move in the direction of their destiny and their calling. God has given us His Word to provide what we need to "be complete, equipped for every good work."[13] As 2 Timothy 3:16 explains, "All Scripture is breathed out by God and profitable for teaching, for reproof, for correction, and for training in right-eousness." God has also given us His Holy Spirit to lead us and guide us into "all the truth."[14] James 1:5 instructs us to "ask God" if we need wisdom. We can go to Him and ask for direction. We can listen to the Holy Spirit, speaking truth to our hearts from the Father. And we can go to His Word for the same. What's more, we can count on God's disciplining us if we are His sons and daughters. The writer to the Hebrews reminded them of an exhortation about God's discipline when he wrote, "My son, do not regard lightly the discipline of the Lord, nor be weary when reproved by him. For the Lord disciplines the one he loves, and chastises every son whom he receives."[15] We can count on God's discipline and direction because we're His kids.

Prayer

Abba, Father, how great is Your love toward us. Long ago, in eternity past, You predestined us to be Your children. Thank You for not only adopting us and giving us a new name, but thank You for giving us life, abundant and eternal. Thank You for all Your provision of food, clothing, and shelter. We're grateful for Your constant protection and care, and for speaking identity and direction over us.

Jesus, we're grateful for the cross, for the blood that You shed so that we could come into the family of God. Thank You for showing us the love of the Father and for being our Elder Brother.

Holy Spirit, thank You for shedding the love of God abroad in our hearts and for leading us and guiding us into all truth. Help us to know the love of the Father at a deeper level. Assure us of our rights and privileges as joint heirs with Jesus.

Reflection

1. In what ways do you still see yourself living with an "orphan mindset"—feeling unworthy, unwanted, or unsure of belonging? How might the Holy Spirit be inviting you to let Him heal those places?

2. As a new creation in Christ, what old ways of thinking about identity or family do you sense God is asking you to address?

3. How have you personally experienced the Holy Spirit teaching you to cry, "Abba, Father"? Where do you sense God drawing you into deeper intimacy and trust?

4. Where can you see evidence of God's DNA, His divine nature, or His transforming work in your life?

5. Where do you feel your identity as a child of God is being challenged or tested right now? How can you anchor yourself in what the Father has spoken over you?

Chapter 6
Identity Defined
and Value Affirmed

Switching schools mid-grade was rough. Doing it twice in five years was simply a compounded difficulty. I changed schools a lot between kindergarten and twelfth grade, and every move was hard—but nothing compared to switching in the middle of the year.

I started out in one school for kindergarten and part of the first grade, then made my first mid-year jump to a new elementary. Then, after finishing first grade, our family moved across state to Grand Rapids, and I began a third school in three years. I continued there from second through fifth grades and moved to the large middle school in that district for sixth grade. At least that transition wasn't completely lonely—some of the kids from my elementary school were there, too, having "graduated" with me from fifth grade. But halfway through sixth grade, I moved again. In the new district, sixth grade was still part of elementary, so I basically had to go from being a middle school dude to an elementary school kid. This was tortuous to my middle school soul.

At best, change is difficult. But being the new kid at school can do great damage to any child's developing sense of identity or self-worth, especially in the child's early stages of formation. I was stressed trying to figure out who I was, how I could fit in with the other kids around me, where to sit during lunch, and how to get other kids to pick me for their teams during sports at recess or in gym class. I still remember that sick feeling we all can get in the pit of our stomachs in situations like these. I was always feeling like an outsider who needed to prove myself.

I'd like to be able to say that the same stress and hurt feelings related to not fitting in or being good enough to be included all went away during high school, but they didn't. I never truly felt like I "fit in" even though I made a few close friends. There was always something nagging me from somewhere in my soul that made me feel like I was "different." It kept me from really diving into some things and made me overreact to others.

The feelings of loneliness and being an outsider continued into college. After graduation, I had hoped I would be chosen to be a young adult leader by my youth pastor. It would have meant that I would be able to stay working in the youth group at church, which had become an important part of my life. It would have also signaled that my pastor, as well as the other leaders, saw a leadership gift and calling to ministry evident in my life. When I wasn't selected, I again felt "unwanted" and began to flounder. I tried to go to the young adult/college and career ministry, but it never really stuck. That had nothing to do with the quality of ministry or the people there. It had everything to do with the internal struggle of my orphan heart. I didn't belong. The sense of calling that I had within me was not affirmed by those who mentored me.

Throughout my high school and college years, I struggled with insecurity and a sense of not being valued. At times, pursuing to understand who I was and whether I mattered to anyone drove me into unhealthy, unsafe, and prodigal directions. I became achievement and performance driven. Even though I had come to a knowledge of Jesus at twelve and ultimately responded to the call of God on my life a few years later, I still had to walk through the process of healing from wounds inflicted in loneliness and discover the love and perfect acceptance of my Heavenly Father. I did begin to mature in my relationship with God the Father and found my identity as a true son. The Father in His goodness directed my way home and embraced me with His affirmation simply because I was and am His son.

Who Am I?

Just as belonging is the primal ache of the human soul, "Who am I?" is the dominant, internal question of the human heart. Knowing and understanding who we are is foundational to our physical, emotional, and mental well-being. The good news is that not only is God able to define and thus reveal to us who we are, but God alone should be the One to do it. Through the finished work of His Son, Jesus, God has redeemed us from our broken identities and given us a brand-new identity as His sons and daughters with full rights and privileges as such.

Your identity is not based on meritocracy, it's not based on you achieving anything, but it's based solely on the mercy of God, and it's accomplished through the finished work of Jesus Christ on the cross. That's good news. Despite that, a lot of us struggle because we know our last names all too well, we know our earthly family and its reputation, and we know the good and the bad that come with being a part of it. So, things can become a little complicated when it comes to believing and embracing God's definition of who we are.

No matter our family name or background, the truth is we all would like to know who we are and, more importantly, who we were meant to be. We're tired of the pipe dreams or best-case scenarios we've made up in our own minds to motivate ourselves. We all want to know who the "real us," including the true reason that we were created and the purpose that our Creator had in mind when we thought us up. We were always meant to be connected to the heart of God because we were destined and created to be children of God. Sin messed that up, but when God is your Father, He alone opens the eyes of your heart and defines for you what your identity is and who He has designed you to become —in Him.

Now, in the last chapter, we spoke about what happens when we receive Christ Jesus as our Savior. John 1:12 explains we have the capacity or power to become God's children. Two things were required for you to enter into a relationship with God through Jesus Christ: (1) You had to believe, and (2) you had to receive. We believe that Jesus is the Son of God. He was sent to the earth by the Father in heaven. He lived sinlessly. He was fully God and fully Man. He went to the cross of Calvary to pay for the sins of the world—for your sins and for my sins. And when we believed in who He is and what He has done, He gave us the legal right to enter into God's family. And when we believe and we receive Christ, the Bible describes what happens to us as being born again. We experience a second birth, a second one into the Kingdom of God and, more specifically, into the family of God.

John 3 recounts a conversation Jesus had with a Pharisee named Nicodemus that addresses the idea of being born again. Not wanting anyone to know what he was doing, Nicodemus went to Jesus to ask Him a few questions. The first thing he said acknowledged his belief that Jesus was a "teacher come from God" because of the signs Jesus did.[1] Jesus, knowing what the visit was really about, cut to the chase and said, "Truly, truly, I say to you, unless one is born again he cannot see the kingdom of God."[2] I'm sure Nicodemus was stunned by Jesus's words because he then asked, "How can a man be born when he is old? Can he enter a second time into His mother's womb and be born?"[3] To that Jesus replied,

> Truly, truly, I say to you, unless one is born of water and the Spirit, he cannot enter the kingdom of God. That which is born of the flesh is flesh, and that which is born of the Spirit is spirit. Do not marvel that I said to you, "You must be born again." The wind blows where it wishes, and you hear its sound, but you do not know where it comes from or where it goes. So it is with everyone who is born of the Spirit.

> — John 3:5–8

Jesus explained that the way into the Kingdom of God is by being born again. When we believe in Him and receive Him as our Savior, Jesus described this as going through a new birth experience. We go from spiritual death to life, coming alive on the inside. God puts His Spirit, His life, and His identity in us. And all those old identities—the labels put on us by others and the ones we thought were our true identities—get exposed at the cross for the frauds that they are. "Well, I thought I was an addict, or I thought I was enough on my own, or I thought I was a good person, or I thought I would be able to figure out who I was myself." All those old identities, the generational ones, the familial ones, even the social ones that we identify with because they give us this false sense of belonging—they all are brought to the foot of the cross and exposed for how weak and how insufficient they really are. When we believe in Jesus, we go through this experience that isn't merely like being born again, but it is a true spiritual rebirth. Through this born-again experience, we enter into the Kingdom of God and into an indestructible relationship with the Father. He, as a father should, teaches us who we are. We learn by revelation and emulation. *We behold the Father and believe what the Father says about us. It is no longer about the identity we think we have within ourselves; it's who we are in Him.*

Do you remember when Jesus was beginning His ministry? We talked about it in the last chapter. He went to the Jordan River where His cousin, John the Baptist, was baptizing people, and He went there specifically to have John baptize Him. Let's look a little more closely at that event. When John baptized Jesus,

> Jesus came up immediately from the water; and behold, the heavens were opened to Him, and He saw the Spirit of God descending like a dove and alighting upon Him. And suddenly a voice came from heaven, saying, "This is My beloved Son, in whom I am well pleased."
>
> — Matthew 3:16–17 NKJV

Think about that. A voice came out of heaven. It was God the Father acknowledging that Jesus was His Son. *You see, sonship must be defined and must be declared by the Father.* Even Jesus, in the days of His humanity, had to go through the process of understanding who He was as the Son of God. Before He could walk as the mature Son and accomplish all that the Father had sent Him for, He needed to receive the affirmation and intimacy of the Father that would secure and fuel Him in His mission.

In the same way, God as a loving father leads each of us through a process of maturity in which we learn our new identity and place as children of God. Undoing old understandings and deceptions and receiving fresh revelation from His Word and the Holy Spirit about our new reality. This is what the Father does. He says, "You're My son. You're My daughter. You're My children." And as 1 Peter 1:3–4 states,

> Blessed be the God and Father of our Lord Jesus Christ! According to his great mercy, he has caused us to be born again, to a living hope through the resurrection of Jesus Christ from the dead, to an inheritance that is imperishable, undefiled, and unfading, kept in heaven for you.

So, we have this identity of being a child of God, born again by His Spirit, with an inheritance kept for us—an inheritance that is enduring and eternal, kept for us in heaven. Wow!

Now, if we look at Romans 6, we read about what water baptism is specifically and why it is very important to us as believers. There are traditional or denominational backgrounds where baptism is something done in infancy as a way of identifying and marking children. What we have practiced throughout the years in the church I've pastored is not infant baptism but infant dedication, where the child's family comes together in the Father's house and commits to training up their child in the Lord. We practice baptizing believers by immersion after they have accepted Jesus as their Lord and Savior and have made a confession of faith. That can happen when they are children or adults, as long as they are capable of making the decision to follow Christ. When I baptize a new believer, I believe something happens that is more than an impartation of grace. *Water baptism is a public funeral and a birth announcement.* It is a circumcision of the heart in which the old Adamic nature is removed. The old identity with Adam and his rebellion is put under the water and left there in a watery grave, but as we come up out of the water, we identify with Jesus, our Elder Brother, who was raised from the grave into marvelous life. This is what the apostle Paul had to say about it in Romans 6:3–11:

> Do you not know that all of us who have been baptized into Christ Jesus were baptized into his death? We were buried therefore with him by baptism into death, in order that, just as Christ was raised from the dead by the glory of the Father, we too might walk in newness of life. For if we have been united with him in a death like his, we shall certainly be united with him in a resurrection like his. We know that our old self was crucified with him in order that the body of sin might be brought to nothing, so that we would no longer be enslaved to sin. For one who has died has been set free from sin. Now if we have died with Christ, we believe that we will also live with him. We know that Christ, being raised from the dead, will never die again; death no longer has dominion over him. For the death that he died, he died to sin once and for all, but the life that he lives he lives to God. So you must also consider yourselves dead to sin and alive to God in Christ Jesus.

What did Paul say happens when we are baptized? We're making a public declaration, an announcement. You see, many of us have gone to funerals and have seen the remains of a friend or loved one being committed to God. But we also show up at showers and hospitals for the birth of a baby. We attend church services where we celebrate the birth and dedicate the child to the Lord. That's why water baptism is both a public funeral and a birth announcement.

Another analogy I like to use is that of a passport. A passport, for example, is one of the most valuable things that, as American citizens, we own. People around the world wish they had a passport from the United States because of the benefits that go along with it and the freedoms as well. I mean, all passports are not the same, right? If you had a passport from a country that had limited rights, you might be very proud of your nation and proud to be who you are as a citizen of that nation, but you still would live limited by the rights of your nation. Your passport will have your picture, your height, the date of issue, and a governmental seal.

When you were born of the flesh, before you were born again, you were born with an Adamic passport. That passport did not have the governmental seal of the Kingdom of God. It did not say, "In Christ." What it said was, "In Adam." What it said was, "In darkness." You were part of the kingdom of darkness, and you were limited as a citizen of the kingdom of darkness and the nation of Adam. That was under a curse, and only the rights of and the enslavement to sin were the privileges that your first passport gave you. All it did was guarantee you slavery and death and a curse. But when you were born again, God became your Father. He incorporated you into His family, taking your old passport out of the kingdom of darkness and Adam and destroying it. He buried your passport in the waters of baptism, and He issued you a brand-new passport that says, "In Christ," or "In the Kingdom of God." That new passport bears a brand-new name. What's more, it never expires, with all the rights and the freedoms and the privileges of eternal life, forgiveness, adoption, salvation, healing, provision, and the blessing of the Father upon your life. That passport can never be taken away. That's what happens when we're saved and baptized.

What are we saved from? We're saved from what we were under the old Adamic curse, and now we've been brought in or translated into the Kingdom of God. Getting baptized is a holy act of faith, of getting in the water, and publicly declaring you know: "I was dead, but now I am alive. I was a citizen of the world and bound under the judgment and the curse of my own sin, but Jesus took it and paid my sin debt in full and has made it possible for me now to become a child of God. I've been born again, I'm a citizen of the Kingdom of heaven, and so now I am publicly standing in the water and burying my old man, my old identity. I'm burying him, and I'm coming up out of the water like Jesus came out of the tomb on the third day, in the newness of life, filled with the Spirit, beloved by the Father. I have a future and a hope. I have a destiny and eternal life. I'm in a family with God the Father. I have a mother, and she's called the Church of Jesus Christ. I have an Elder Brother named Jesus who has made a way for me to come into the family. I have the Holy Spirit, my Intercessor and the Power of heaven, living inside me, and nothing can separate me from the love of God!"

All our earthly identities are buried with Jesus, and we come up out of the waters of baptism into the newness of life with a brand-new identity in Christ, with the Father speaking over us, "This is My beloved son, in whom I am well pleased. This is My beloved daughter, in whom I'm well pleased." If Jesus Christ is truly the Lord of your life, if you've really been born again, you've repented of your old identities, and you've traded them in for your brand-new passport in the Kingdom of God, then you have access to all that the Father has provided for you. The Father no longer sees your past dirty and sin-stained identity. He doesn't look at you and remember all the mistakes you made. Those have all been washed away by the blood of Jesus. All the Father sees is His spotless, holy, blameless, son or daughter, and He is speaking blessing over your life. Isn't that good? It's so good that it's great!

Yet, in Christ, we're no longer free agents. We aren't left to ourselves. That's what a free agent is, someone on their own doing whatever they want. In Christ Jesus, we aren't free agents, but we are redeemed. *Redeemed* is a New Testament word that Paul the apostle used. When he used the word, he was thinking about slave markets. He was thinking about people who had been enslaved, indentured, and owned by someone else. Paul was thinking about slaves who had been dragged down to markets, stripped in humiliating fashion, and naked, being inspected by people who wanted to purchase them. According to Paul, this is what happens to us in our own sin, as citizens of darkness. Under sin, our old identities, we were enslaved to sin, to our passions, to that internal fire that burns and combusts—the one we couldn't control, the one we knew was wrong and couldn't fix. That old sinful identity enslaved us and humiliated us, stripping us of our human dignity and the image of God that we were created to bear. And there we were in the slave market with the enemy, the devil. He had us tethered in chains. He had legal right in our sin to abuse and take advantage of us. He deceived us and manipulated us. But one day, a Man came to the slave market. He saw us broken, scarred, worn, and abused. He asked, "How much for this one here?" And the devil answered, "Your life for his." And Jesus said, "I'll pay it."

Jesus then took the slave's place, allowing His own kingly garments to be stripped off Him in a humiliating fashion. He was abused, mocked, ridiculed, and murdered so that the slave could be set free. That transaction is what it means to be redeemed, to be set free. As part of this new identity that is ours in Christ, we are not our own anymore. We have been bought with a price. We are the redeemed of God.

Am I Valued?

No one is born knowing their inherent value.[4] We form this perception over time based on how we are seen and treated by the people in our lives, most critically, by our primary caregivers. In other words, self-worth isn't developed in a vacuum. It functions as a social barometer. Oh, we have tracking, how we're doing in the eyes of others, and that becomes the story we tell ourselves about how much we are valued by those around us. It's a social barometer. It's this desire, this innate desire, that drives us as we keep evaluating ourselves by it. "How am I doing? Do I fit in? Do they really like me? Are my friends really my friends or not?" It's why loneliness is one of the driving factors of emotional unwell-being in young people, and why anxiety is plaguing an entire generation. One of the leading causes of depression and even suicide is this sense of having tried unsuccessfully to fit in and belong.

The apostle Paul wrote to the Corinthian church that was filled with people who had come out of paganism, idolatry, immorality, wealth, and influence in a great old Roman culture. They also were very familiar with the language of redemption because they had their own slaves or were simply familiar with the slave markets. So, when Paul asked in 1 Corinthians 6:19, "Do you not know that your body is a temple of the Holy Spirit within you, whom you have from God?" In other words, they had been born again. They were not their own. Wait a second. The world says, "You do you," or "Be your best version of yourself." But Paul was writing to believers who understood slave markets. He was telling them they were not their own. They had been bought with a price. They had been redeemed. He was reminding them of that fact.

As one of those who have been redeemed, I want to remind you that God didn't only change your identity when He redeemed you. Jesus paid the price to purchase you back. He determined and affirmed your value long before He set you free and made you fully alive. It was His life for yours. He affirmed your value when He died for you while you were yet dead in your identity as a sinner. His redemption—the blood that He shed, the nails in His hands and feet, the crown of thorns, all His suffering—said you are worth it. If you've ever wondered how much you are worth in God's sight, all you have to do is look at the cross and see the price Jesus was willing to pay. The wounds are His receipts forever of the fact that God the Father was willing to bankrupt heaven in order to redeem you back to Himself.

The price the Father paid for your redemption—the blood of His Son, Jesus—gave you a new identity, gave you value you never knew you had, and transferred you into His Kingdom forever. You have a new passport and an imperishable inheritance.

Beloved, are you walking through this life with your new passport, or are you still trying to make it on your old one? Your new passport was issued to you after you were saved and baptized. Everything changed when you were given your new identity. Your citizenship is different. Yours is now a heavenly citizenship.[5] You're simply a sojourner or exile here on Earth.[6] This is not your home, but are you still walking around with your old passport as a slave to sin? Maybe the old picture in your old passport of how you used to look is affecting the way you're living today.

What did Paul say? We come up out of the water and into our new identity. Why? So we can walk in newness of life. In other words, the Father wants us to live differently. Listen, when you have a brand-new identity, everything changes. But if you're walking around with your old passport and you get into a situation where you're struggling with your identity or with your self-worth, all you have to do is look at the cross. What was the price of your redemption? Jesus's blood for you. What does this blood say about you? Better things than anything out of your past.

Ephesians 1:5 tells you that you were chosen by God. You weren't tolerated by Him. You're now holy and blameless. You're not stained by sin anymore. You've been adopted into God's family. You've not been rejected and left as an orphan any longer. You're accepted, not rejected. You're redeemed, no longer a slave. And the price that was paid for you is the value of Jesus's blood, God's own Son, and God willingly paid it. And at the end of the day, what does God give to us? He has not poured out judgment, condemnation, anger, or frustration. Ephesians 1:8 explains God has lavished His blood, love, and forgiveness upon us. He has not sprinkled them or rationed them. No, He has *lavished* His blood, love, and forgiveness upon you and me.

Do you know that, if you are in Christ, God's no longer looking at you through your good days or your bad days, through your best efforts? He isn't waiting on you to earn anything. Everything has been paid for. He sees you now through the rose-colored glasses of Jesus's blood, and when He sees you, He sees Jesus. When He sees you, He sees spotless. When He sees you, He sees forgiven. When He sees you, He doesn't see the pauper with an old passport. He sees the prince or the princess seated with Christ in heavenly places, with robes of righteousness on, with a ring of the family on your finger, and with a new way of living, sandals on your feet, and a sword of the Spirit in your hand. He sees your name written in the Lamb's Book of Life, an internal destiny before you. And nothing in this world, nothing above, nothing beneath, nothing in your past, nothing in the future, nothing in heaven, nothing in hell, or nothing in your own mind can separate you ever from His love, and that is the good news of the gospel.

Prayer

Father, thank You for Your goodness. Thank You for Your mercy upon mercy and Your grace upon grace. Thank You for Jesus and His precious redeeming blood. I am amazed at what You have done for me in sending me Jesus, in changing my identity, and in declaring my value. Thank You for lavishing Your love upon me. I love You, Father.

Thank You, Jesus, for taking my place, for dying for me, for shedding Your blood. I desire to no longer walk as a free agent but as one who has been redeemed.

Holy Spirit, remind me of my identity in Christ and what He did for me. Free me from walking in my old identity. May I no longer look to others for my identity or value. Help me to be ever mindful that I am a child of God and that He forever loves me.

Reflection

1. In what ways has your childhood shaped your sense of identity and self-worth?

2. How does knowing that identity is something God gives —not something we earn—challenge or comfort you?

3. What is the significance of baptism being described as both a funeral and a birth announcement?

4. How does understanding you've been "bought with a price" deepen your sense of value and self-worth?

5. What voices or experiences have most shaped your understanding of your value? How does Scripture correct or confirm them?

Chapter 7
Vulnerability Protected

Within the first six to seven years of our lives, we develop the deep-seated operating system of what we believe about ourselves, the world, and other people. That means our senses of identity, security, and emotional safety are all forming during these critical years.

Since I didn't have my life-changing encounter with God until I was twelve years of age, I had a lot of internal beliefs that weren't rooted in God's truth but in the opinions of those around me and in how they treated me. What was especially difficult to bear was the shame, guilt, and trauma associated with sexual abuse, which I experienced at a very young age from an older relative, a babysitter, and a few older kids in my neighborhood.

I don't know who may have said this, but the heart of a child can be compared to a lint roller, picking up everything it comes into contact with. My heart was that vulnerable as a child. My heart picked up all kinds of stuff from my environment because, like any other child, I was extremely sensitive to my surroundings.

That sensitivity shaped me in ways I didn't even know until later in life. Whatever that lint roller picked up provided information for my internal operating system. It became the programming in my heart that left me even more vulnerable to the choices and voices of others.

Vulnerability is the quality or state of being exposed to the possibility of being attacked or harmed, either physically or emotionally. No one wants to be vulnerable. In fact, we all fear being found out or being vulnerable because, when we're vulnerable, nothing stands between us and the rest of the world. The very possibility of embarrassment, of rejection, of betrayal, or of physical injury becomes more probable when we are unprotected.

I remember the confusion that I felt as a small boy after being sexually abused by those I looked up to. Neighbor boys that were much older than I—guys I wanted to accept me—took advantage of my innocence and that longing to be accepted. A relative who had been entrusted with taking care of me sometimes left me with shame after he touched me inappropriately. The emotions I felt as a result of the abuse were emotions that no child (or anyone, for that matter) should ever have to experience. The grand larceny of lust imposed upon the innocent is one of the most tragic sins I can think of because, once the things are awakened in a young heart as a result, they can never be undone or put back. The Bible speaks about not awakening love before it's time.[1] In no way am I calling child sexual abuse "love," but in a much broader sense, the awakening of sexual reality within a child creates an awareness and feelings that they are not at all equipped to handle. That was my story.

The abuse as a small, vulnerable boy combined with the exposure to pornography by my biological father set me in a place where I would never not be aware of sex. I had been robbed of childhood innocence and left clothed with filthy garments of sexual shame. It would take the grace of God and the love of the Father to undo the damage to my soul later in my life so that I could walk in freedom and be "unashamed." *When God is our Father, He promises to protect our vulnerability.*

Hiding Behind Leaves and Trees

Once we've become exposed and vulnerable, we resort to what our earthly forefathers did: We hide behind leaves and trees. Adam and Eve were in the lush and safe environs of the garden of Eden, the perfect place God had created for them to live and commune with Him. Genesis 1 retells for us the creation story of the heavens, the earth, and everything in them, including man. We're told that everything God made "was very good."[2]

In Genesis 2, the wide lens storytelling of Genesis 1 specifically and telescopically focuses on God's creation of man in His image. Verse 7 explains, "Then the Lord God formed the man of dust from the ground and breathed into his nostrils the breath of life, and the man became a living creature."

God planted a garden there in Eden and placed man in it. There were plenty of leaves and trees in this garden as we're told that God "made to spring up every tree" that was a delight to behold and that was "good for food."[3] The Tree of Life as well as the Tree of the Knowledge of Good and Evil were also in the garden. Not wanting Adam to dwell alone in the garden,

> The Lord God caused a deep sleep to fall upon the man, and while he slept took one of his ribs and closed up its place with flesh. And the rib that the Lord God had taken from the man he made into a woman and brought her to

the man. Then the man said, "This at last is bone of my bones and flesh of my flesh; she shall be called Woman, because she was taken out of Man."

— Genesis 2:21–23

After God created Eve, He performed the first marriage bringing Eve to Adam. Verses 24–25 pronounce their marriage with these words, "Therefore a man shall leave his father and his mother and hold fast to his wife, and they shall become one flesh. And the man and his wife were both naked and were not ashamed."

Naked and unashamed, the couple were given one command that allowed for them to eat the fruit of all the trees except one: the Tree of the Knowledge of Good and Evil.[4] Many people have questioned, "Why would God put a tree in the garden and not let them eat from it? Was it to tempt them?" No, God placed the tree with the "forbidden fruit" as a test of trust. We know according to Genesis 3:6 that Eve saw the fruit was good and ate it after being duped by the serpent liar, the devil. She, we discover in 2 Corinthians 11:3, was deceived by the "cunning" of the devil. Eve, then, gave the fruit to Adam, who also ate of it. First Timothy 2:14 attests, "Adam was not deceived, but the woman was deceived and became a transgressor." Both Adam and Eve violated the trust and failed the test that God had given to them. All relationships are based on trust. When trust is there, the relationship is strong. When trust is broken, covenant is broken.

Once the couple ate the fruit, Genesis 3:7 lets us know that their eyes "were opened, and they knew that they were naked." For the very first time in their existence in the garden, Adam and Eve knew that they were exposed. And so, what did they do? "They sewed fig leaves together and made for themselves loincloths." Because of their sin and their rejection of God and His truth, what the enemy did was he opened their eyes or he gave them an understanding of something that they didn't know before in their innocence—that they were then totally exposed and totally naked. With their innocence lost, they stood unguarded and exposed. Their response was the same response any of us would have had. Exposed, they began to take whatever was available to them, making coverings for themselves in order to protect themselves from their vulnerability. When "they heard the sound of the Lord walking in the garden in the cool of the day," they hid from God's Presence "among the trees of the garden."[5]

What had God warned them about when He commanded them not to eat of the Tree of the Knowledge of Good and Evil? He had said, "For in the day that you eat of it you shall surely die."[6] *The way that death began to manifest itself right after the first couple sinned was through fear, guilt, and shame.* If death is the absence of life, and life is the Presence of God, then their breach of trust left them slowly experiencing the impact of death on multiple levels.

Genesis 5:5 says that Adam was 930 years old when he died. Though the Bible doesn't say how old Eve was when she died, different traditions place her death somewhere between shortly after Adam's death and fifty to sixty years after it. The point is neither of them died immediately after they sinned. Nevertheless, death entered into them physically, spiritually, and emotionally the moment that they violated God's command. From then on, death would work in them, in their relationships, and in their descendants throughout all generations. Death would even work its way into the rest of creation.

In the aftermath of their sin, Adam and Eve made loincloths for themselves. Let's look for a moment at the word *loincloths*, translated from the Hebrew word *chagor* or *chagorah*. The Hebrew word means a covering or some sort of a protection used to cover the most vulnerable parts of a person's body. The loincloths Adam and Eve made for themselves were meant to cover their nakedness. Theirs was an attempt to protect themselves from what would have been their first experiences ever of feelings of embarrassment, fear, guilt, and shame.

Can you remember the first time you experienced any of these feelings? What was your first reaction? I can remember wanting to run and hide. In fact, we've all heard someone, after suffering some kind of wardrobe malfunction in public or some other personally embarrassing situation, say something like, "Where can I go and hide my face? I wish the ground would open up and swallow me. I want to crawl into a hole and disappear. Just let me curl up and die!" The emotional exposure and vulnerability can be the most fearful thing that can happen in the human experience. It's one of the reasons many individuals dread public speaking, for example—because they're afraid that they could mess up, say something wrong, and be mocked or laughed at by others. It's that fear of exposure that makes public speaking very off-putting.

Adam's and Eve's fear of exposure to the world was one thing, but their very felt need of protecting their vulnerabilities of who they then were caused them to want to put something between the Father and themselves. We do the same with our vulnerabilities today. We take fig leaves and cover ourselves in our relationships with other people, and then we find trees that we hide behind to protect ourselves from God. Can I tell you that, our trying to cover ourselves and hide isn't only physical, but it's also emotional, it's also spiritual, and it's connected to the deepest part of who we are?

We cover up with fig leaves, with other things, because we're afraid that, if the most vulnerable, real part of us is ever exposed, it will produce rejection and embarrassment and guilt and shame.

What happens to us because of these things is we become afraid to allow people to see the "real us" with all our issues. We're afraid to be who we truly are and allow people in emotionally because we're afraid that, somehow, we're so different or more broken or more needy than they. No one wants to put themselves out there only to be made a fool of. This fear of others seeing us as we really are, without any shield or masks, makes us fear being rejected and deemed "defective." If we tell them the whole story of our lives, they will walk away from us.

Yet it's in our sharing with God and others the vulnerabilities of our lives that we can find healing. Sadly, we spend much of our lives sewing fig leaves together to cover the areas of our emotional vulnerability so that we can survive. Behind those leaves, though, fear, shame, and guilt remain. This is what happens. This is why we project a certain image to the world and even to our co-workers, family, and friends. We know what's expected of us, so we sew a costume of fig leaves made up of things of this world that will give us the acceptance of others. We hide behind the trees of this world, hoping to protect ourselves from the judgmental gazes of people. After all, letting someone into our lives, allowing them to live all up close and personal, requires a high level of trust. If you get married, for example, you're letting down your guard and being vulnerable. You're sharing all your fears, your mistakes, your idiosyncrasies, your triggers, and your trauma because you've trusted somebody in the context of covenant. But for so many of us, we continue to keep people at a distance, including our spouses.

I, for example, was married for several years before I shared with my wife, Jane, the sexual abuse I experienced as a child. *The truth is we can live our whole lives and never deal with the shame and never deal with the pain, never deal with our hurts, never confront our sins, and we can truly never be ourselves.* We simply work hard maintaining our hiddenness by sewing leaves and making loincloths and living among the trees.

The greatest tragedy for a human being is to live their entire life as somebody else, as the person they think other people want them to be, and never live as their true self, the person God wanted them to be. We live our whole lives with fig leaves, false identities, false images, portraying ourselves as the guy or gal who's got it all together, got it all figured out. We project this false image of being disciplined and organized, of having wealth and possessions, all the while we're bleeding and wounded inside. We're insecure and scared. And so, we gather up thousands of followers on Instagram, depicting a false persona and broadcasting a life in pics, posts, and reels, which is how we cover ourselves in leaves and hide among the trees. We're Instagram perfect, but inside we're dying as death is at work in fear, guilt, and shame.

How many times have we heard about a friend from high school or a celebrity we thought had it all together only to find out that their lives are not anything like their image? Unfortunately, we've heard all too often about those whose fear of being found out or trauma or shame became so great they committed suicide. We had no idea about the pain that they were experiencing. It's because of fig leaves. They sewed together these fig leaves. And can I tell you that the enemy of your soul is content with you living a fig-leaf life? He's fine with it because you're not living the true life God originally designed for you. You're on the outside looking green and flourishing and alive. On the inside, you're dying. You're holding everyone at a distance behind those fig leaves or trees, and you're doing the same to God.

Think about some of the trees that we all use to hide ourselves from God. *We hide behind the tree of ritual, where we replace inti-*

mate relationship with some sort of traditional observance. You might call that religion. Religion isn't a bad word unless it's void of intimate relationship. Sometimes, we can go through the motions. This is what the Pharisees did. They prayed the right prayers, they memorized the right scriptures, they looked the part, they honored the Sabbath, they didn't eat anything unclean, but Jesus said to them, "Woe to you, scribes and Pharisees, hypocrites! For you are like whitewashed tombs, which outwardly appear beautiful, but within are full of dead people's bones and all uncleanness."[7] He basically told them they looked good on the outside, but on the inside, they had nothing but death, hiding behind a tree of ritual.

Think about rebellion. *We hide behind a tree of rebellion where we simply run from God.* How many people have grown up in church in our culture, have grown up in Sunday school, yet because in some part of their hearts or minds they know that they've chosen a path that's not pleasing to God? So, what do they do? They run harder and faster and further away from God.

We also hide behind the tree of good works. We act like we're good people doing good works, but really what we're trying to do is we're trying to merit or earn permission to come out from behind the trees. Once we've made ourselves good enough, kind of like hopping into a dressing room and getting fitted with some nice clothing, we're willing to come out from behind the trees because we've made ourselves look nice. How many times have we heard someone say, "I'll come to church once I get my life together"? We try to do the right things for God thinking then we'll be acceptable to Him. Meanwhile, God's like, "Where are you? Do you not see that you're desperate? Do you not see that you're exposed, that I can see all the things that you think you're hiding? Your good works are filthy rags." "Our righteousness," the Bible says, is as "filthy rags."[8]

We may even hide behind a tree of reverse blame. What's that? It's where we hide behind the tree because we refuse to acknowledge our guilt, our shame, or our fear, and we blame God. We hide to punish God. We distance ourselves from Him because of the things that He has done or for the things that He hasn't done that we thought He should have done. And God says the same thing to us that He said to Adam, "Where are you?" In other words, "Find yourself on the GPS. Locate your current location. You're far away from Me. You're vulnerable, and you think you're protected, but you're actually exposed." Beloved, only God can cover you. Only God can cover your shame, your guilt, and your fear. Only God can cover your vulnerability.

The Father's Response

Looking back at the account, while Adam and Eve were hiding from God, the Lord called out to Adam, "Where are you?"[9] Adam's response is very telling. "He said, 'I heard the sound of you in the garden, and I was afraid, because I was naked, and I hid myself.'"[10] Every single day, "in the cool of the day," the Father would come into the garden to commune or fellowship with them. This particular day was no different except, instead of the couple coming out to meet the Father, He had to call out to them. As a father, He wanted to hear about their day, to check on them, and to interact with them. Could you imagine how different this day must have been for Adam and Eve? Before they sinned, they would have looked forward to this special time with God. Perhaps, He would teach them about things or share knowledge with them. Or maybe they would have told Him of some new experience they had in the garden. But because Adam and Eve knew that they had betrayed and disobeyed God, the reality of their nakedness made them find a way to distance themselves from the gaze of and the conversation with the One who created them and loved them.

"Adam, where are you? Eve, where are you?" I don't think God had to ask those questions because He knows all and He sees all, but He was calling Adam and Eve back to Himself, back to relationship, back to accountability. God called out to them for their sake. He wanted the couple to see where their choices had taken them. "Where are you?" The Maker of the trees called to the couple hiding among the trees. It was insanity. "I'm the One who loves you, I'm your Father, but now you've allowed shame and guilt to cover you." The voice of the Lord is supposed to attract us, draw us to Him, but because of so much of our shame and our guilt, things that we've done, things that we're embarrassed of, all our inadequacies, they've made us feel like we're not enough. We think, *I'm not spiritual enough. I don't know enough about the Bible. I'm struggling emotionally. You don't know my past. You don't know the times that I've turned and I've said I'm going to do the right thing. But I've done the wrong thing over and over again.* And now we have this fear and are repulsed away from the Lord. And God asks us the same question, "Where are you?"

The beauty of this very sad, heartbreaking situation is the response of the Father: "And the Lord God made for Adam and for his wife garments of skins and clothed them."[11] The word for *clothe* in this verse is a root Hebrew word from which we get the word *atone*. The word *atone* means to cover or to clothe. The Father's response to clothe and cover Adam and Eve is the first mention in the Scriptures of the idea of God providing atonement for our sins. God the Father made skins to cover the first couple for their sin.

Do you know that, for God to make an outfit of skins for Adam and Eve, something had to die, something's blood had to be shed for them to have a covering? Life had to be given for Adam and Eve to have a covering. God Himself went and provided a garment or a covering, a true atonement, over their shame and their guilt and their sin. It was His action that brought about protecting them in their vulnerability. It was God's initiative, and this is the good news, because only God can cover us. Only God can really provide redemption for us from the things from which we feel guilt and shame. Only God can redeem us from our emotional brokenness and the trauma of our pasts. Only God can do this.

Thankfully for us, God loves to heal and to cover. God loves to cover our vulnerabilities. Psalm 32:1–2 says, "Blessed is the one whose transgression is forgiven, whose sin is covered. Blessed is the man against whom the Lord counts no iniquity, and in whose spirit there is no deceit." And why would God love and desire to cover us? Because, as Psalm 103:13–14 tells us, "As a father shows compassion to his children, so the Lord shows compassion to those who fear him. For he knows our frame; he remembers that we are dust." The fatherly heart of God—the compassion of the Father—is what moves God. Compassion is what moved Jesus to forgive sins. Remember Jesus is the perfect revelation of the Father. Why does God forgive sins? Because we deserve it. No, the Bible tells us it's the compassion of God that moves Him to forgive sin. Why does God heal? Because He is compassionate. Why does God cover our vulnerabilities? It's because He has compassion as our Father. God knows our frame. He knows us more intimately than we know ourselves. This is why it's silly to hide behind trees. This is why it's silly to think somehow we can fake God out.

I can remember my teen years and how I hid behind the fig leaves of performance, excelling in art and athleticism. I was trying to put up fig leaves to protect myself from being laughed at, embarrassed, and exposed because if people really knew the pain that I felt on the inside, if people really knew what had been done to me that I dare not tell anybody, then they would have rejected me, they would have turned me away, and I would have been left alone. But it took God, it took Jesus, it took the work of the Father revealing Himself to me, calling out to me and then covering me because of His great compassion. I discovered Psalm 27:10 became a reality for me—that even if my mother and my father forsake me, "the Lord will take me in." I realized that He is truly the "Father of the fatherless."[12] My dad came back around, and we ended up having a great relationship. My biological father received the Lord. He got saved. He was an amazing grandfather. I'm so grateful for him. And years later, my stepdad did. He is an amazing man. I'm so grateful for his role in my life. It wasn't their fault that I had my own shame and guilt and trauma, but it was the Lord's doing to step in and to heal that. For the Father to step in and say, "Lee, you can take down your fig leaves. You don't have to hide behind trees anymore."

You see, one of the greatest promises that the Father gives to us is God promises us ten times in the Scriptures that He, unlike anybody else, will never leave us and He will never forsake us. Ten is the number of perfection and completeness. We need to look at these promises for a moment:

1. Genesis 28:15 says, "'Behold, I am with you and will keep you wherever you go, and will bring you back to this land. For I will not leave you until I have done what I have promised.'"

2. Deuteronomy 4:31 declares, "'For the Lord your God is a merciful God. He will not leave you or destroy you or

forget the covenant with your fathers that he swore to them.'"

3. Deuteronomy 31:6 tells us, "'Be strong and courageous. Do not fear or be in dread of them, for it is the Lord your God who goes with you. He will not leave you or forsake you.'"

4. Deuteronomy 31:8 promises, "'It is the Lord who goes before you. He will be with you; he will not leave you or forsake you. Do not fear or be dismayed.'"

5. Joshua 1:5 declares, "'Just as I was with Moses, so I will be with you. I will not leave you or forsake you.'"

6. Joshua 1:9 states, "'Have I not commanded you? Be strong and courageous. Do not be frightened, and do not be dismayed, for the Lord your God is with you wherever you go.'"

7. 1 Chronicles 28:20 says, "Then David said to Solomon his son, 'Be strong and courageous and do it. Do not be afraid and do not be dismayed, for the Lord God, even my God, is with you. He will not leave you or forsake you.'"

8. Matthew 28:20 promises, "'Behold, I am with you always, to the end of the age.'"

9. John 14:18 proclaims, "'I will not leave you as orphans; I will come to you.'"

10. Hebrews 13:5–6 says, "For he has said, 'I will never
     leave you nor forsake you.' So we can confidently say,
     'The Lord is my helper; I will not fear; what can man do
     to me?'"

God promised to Abraham, Israel, Joshua, Solomon, the disciples, and us that He will never leave us or abandon us. He will
cover and protect our vulnerability. You and I don't have to hide
behind fig leaves and trees any longer when God is our Father.

You know, it truly breaks my heart to see a generation that has
all this shame and guilt—all this anxiety and worry about the
future—hiding behind their social media fig leaves. Or they're
hiding behind some cause that they can grab ahold of that gives
them a feeling of significance and importance. Or they're hiding
behind intellectualism and their degree and their earning money,
or their position or their angst toward society. None of these things
will cover our vulnerability. All these things do is mask our deep-
seated pain.

But God offers us atonement. He offers us cover. Why does God
cover us? It's because He cares for us and knows our frame.
Romans 5:8 says, "But God shows his love for us in that while we
were still sinners, Christ died for us." Think about that. When we
were without strength or ability to save ourselves, when we didn't
have the ability to cover our sin and our shame, Jesus did it for us.
I love how the Message communicates this truth in Romans 5:6–9:

Christ arrives right on time to make this happen. He didn't,
and doesn't, wait for us to get ready. He presented himself
for this sacrificial death when we were far too weak and
rebellious to do anything to get ourselves ready. And even if
we hadn't been so weak, we wouldn't have known what to

do anyway. We can understand someone dying for a person worth dying for, and we can understand how someone good and noble could inspire us to selfless sacrifice. But God put his love on the line for us by offering his Son in sacrificial death.

Because of God's great compassion, because of the love of the Father, He covers our vulnerability.

Jesus is our covering. He is our eternal atonement. Matthew 27:31 says, "And when they had mocked him, they stripped him of the robe and put his own clothes on him and led him away to crucify him." Jesus was fully exposed for us. He was whipped, beaten, and exposed so that we could be covered. All we have to do is look at Jesus, who is the perfect picture of the Father. If you look at what Jesus did on the cross, it's a perfect solution and antidote to what man did in the garden. What was part of the curse? Genesis 3:18 said the ground would produce "thorns and thistles." Jesus's crown was made of thorns. Why? Because Jesus took the curse off the land and off the anxiety and toil of working by the sweat of our brows—sweat because of anxiety and worry about the future. Jesus took it. His hands were pierced. Why? Because our hands have committed sin and Jesus was pierced to remove the guilt of our actions. His feet were pierced. Why? Because all of us have walked on the path of the sinner, but Jesus allowed His feet to be pierced so that ours could be cleaned. And His side was pierced that revealed water and blood pouring out of His heart. Why did Jesus do that? Jesus's heart literally was broken so that our broken hearts could be healed.

Jesus was exposed on the front side of the tree, the very tree that you and I had been hiding behind. You see, when the Father said, "Where are you?" it took 4,000 years for the Son to walk toward that tree and find all of us hiding behind it. Instead of shaming us and condemning us, Jesus allowed Himself to be stripped and made vulnerable, and to be crucified on that tree, so that we could be covered by His blood and His sacrifice and be made whole. This is what Jesus meant when He said, "I am the way, and the truth, and the life. No one comes to the Father except through me."[13] Hallelujah! Through Jesus, there is a new and living way for us to boldly come before the throne of grace in our time of need.[14]

Jesus comes to heal our most vulnerable places, the places that we think we've covered. He sees us, and He doesn't reject us. The Father says to us today, "If you'll bring that to Me"—whatever it is —"I will cover you. I will heal you. I will forgive you. You don't have to earn it. My Son, Jesus, paid for it, and I will give you robes of righteousness for your nakedness. I will give you the oil of gladness. Where there have been ashes of destruction, come to Me. I am the only One. I am your Father, and to as many as received Jesus, I have given them the ability to be called sons and daughters of God."

Prayer

Heavenly Father, today, I'm surrendering. I'm waving the white flag, Father. I ask You to forgive me for hiding from You, for trying to sew together fig leaves to cover my own vulnerability. Thank You for sending Your Son to die on the tree I've been hiding behind.

Jesus, thank You for showing me the love of the Father and for making atonement for my brokenness. I believe You died for me, paid for my sin and my shame, and I believe You rose again to give me eternal life. From this day forward, I surrender to You, Lord. I will no longer hide. I will no longer try to cover cover my vulnerability.

Holy Spirit, remind me of all that Jesus has accomplished for me. Lead me and guide me out from behind the things I typically go to for cover. Thank You.

Reflection

1. How do you define vulnerability?

2. Describe some situations in your life where you fear being "exposed" emotionally or spiritually.

3. What "fig leaves" (e.g., image, performance, humor, perfectionism, people-pleasing, anger, etc.) do you tend to sew together to protect yourself?

4. What is your response to God when He calls you near in moments that you're thriving? What is your response to Him when He calls to you in moments that you feel ashamed or inadequate?

5. What would it look like, practically speaking, to live as someone who believes their vulnerability is protected because God is their Father?

Chapter 8
Orphaned No More

I thought about things as a kid that no child should ever have to think about. Between the ages of ten and twelve, bruised by different traumas of my childhood, I frequently withdrew to my room and sat there for hours, struggling with my identity, trying to figure out where I fit in, and looking for the ever-elusive happiness others seemed to have. I was artistic, creative, insecure, and introverted, which didn't help me bond readily with others. Yet there were two people, my grandfather and grandmother, who served as a safe harbor for me.

Before my tween years, before Mom married Bob, my grandparents allowed my mother and me to live with them for a couple of years, helping Mom get back on her feet after Dad had left. My grandparents were joyful lovers of Jesus. They were devout Pentecostals. And when we went to church with them, we were there a long time, some three to four hours. Much time was given to preaching, testifying, singing, and "tarrying." I remember watching my grandmother play the Hammond B3 organ in those services. She had a beehive hairdo, so when "the Holy Ghost came," as old-time Pentecostals used to say, I always knew because my grandmother's high-nested hair would cast a twitching shadow against the church wall. Her hair wasn't the only signal that God had come into the sanctuary. Even I could sense His Presence there at their church in Clarkston, Michigan.

I don't remember a moment in my life when I did not believe in God or did not have a deep, deep interest in the things of God because my grandparents instilled it in me. Something happened in 1983 when I was staying with them for the summer that changed everything. Rather than merely believing in and admiring God the Father, I had an encounter with Him that led to me becoming a son.

Sunday night on August 7, I reluctantly went to church with my grandparents. There were about fifteen people in the service, and I was a good four decades younger than anyone else there. Nothing profound occurred during worship. Nothing memorable was said during the sermon. But after the message, we were invited to come to the front of the church, and we were encouraged to form a circle, hold hands, and pray.

I remember staring at the ceiling while people began to pray. I heard people intercede for healing for generic needs as well as other requests. Of course, there were names mentioned of people needing salvation. Slowly, I started to lose interest and check out, my eyes tracing the stained ceiling tiles above me. That's when I suddenly became aware of God's Presence. He graciously stepped into my life, the life of a wounded, lost, and fearful kid. In that small church, standing in the small circle of believers, I saw all the pain moments of my life come together. And for the first time, things started to make sense. I realized even in the moments when I felt abandoned, alone, and orphaned, I was never truly alone. God had always been with me.

That night, the Father spoke to me, calling me by name. He spoke powerfully within me in a way that seemed as if the whole world should have been able to hear it, but in reality, only I could. He said, "I have called you to be a voice to your generation and prepare to serve Me." I felt like I was going to explode from the inside out, overwhelmed by the great joy of feeling found and loved. That night, I knew I was orphaned no more. I became a son of God the Father, and this set my life on a trajectory toward my purpose, destiny, and calling.

What It Means to Be an Orphan

Though I belonged to a family that clothed, fed, and nurtured me, I struggled with an orphan mentality. As you know, I wasn't an orphan by definition, but I felt abandoned in some ways. And I think this can be a common feeling experienced by those who were raised in families by one or both biological parents yet were disappointed, let down, rejected, or even abandoned emotionally by their parent or parents. A *de facto* orphan, however, lives a very different life from that of a son or daughter nurtured in a family. The most obvious distinction is the complete absence of parents. The parents may be dead or unknown. They may have simply abandoned the child, leaving the child without any pathway home. Orphans are not only without parents, but they often suffer from multiple psychological disorders, such as anxiety, depression, and PTSD, which create issues of trust and attachment. Loneliness can often be their sole companion.

Over the years, I've had several opportunities to speak with people who either have come out of the old system of orphanages or the more recent foster care system. I've heard various stories of their spending most of their childhood, youth, and even young adulthood in self-dependency. Without a father or mother to care for and protect them, they've had to fend for themselves even within the societal framework that was meant to help them. This self-dependency or self-protection has caused them to isolate as they've been fearful of being harmed or taken advantage of. They've learned from the wounds they've received from the abuse of others and from the failures of others to meet their needs that they can't trust anyone except themselves. As a result, they've also learned that the only voice they can trust, the voice that helps them know how to protect and defend themselves, is the voice of fear. *In a very real sense, orphans can become slaves to fear, and not only when they were children. Their bondage to fear can last well into their adulthood.*

In Ancient Rome, the number one occupation of an orphan was slavery. If a child did not have any extended family—aunts, uncles, grandparents, or cousins—to take them into their homes, slavery was their only option. There wasn't a safety net system for them like foster care. There was adoption, but it wasn't sentimental, meaning it wasn't driven by a compassionate or emotional desire to care, take in, and nurture a child. More often, it served as a legal mechanism for the continuation of a family name or estate.[1]

Relationships in the Roman Empire could be reshaped or reconfigured for the adopter's purposes. If someone with property, means, or title didn't have an heir, that person could adopt a child or even an adult to inherit their estate. Most of the time, if a child was orphaned, that child would not be adopted but would be sold into slavery or be left bereft to die from hunger, thirst, or exposure to the elements.

Interestingly, one of the earliest distinguishing marks of Christians in the Roman Empire—and one of the key ways the Church grew and the gospel advanced in the first and the second centuries —was how Christians cared for and ministered to those marginalized in society (i.e., slaves, women, and orphans). In fact, Christians were known to retrieve abandoned or unwanted children from the streets, woods, or cesspits. Christians would begin to raise these orphaned ones in their homes as their own. Christians would later become the first to develop orphanages.

Yet, in ancient and biblical times, for those orphans who became slaves, their lives continued to be subjugated to fear. They worried about facing punishment or death for not pleasing their masters. Everything they did was driven by performance or fear. The reason why I'm illustrating this picture is because there is an intimate connection between what the Bible talks about orphans and slaves, and how we lived before we received Christ as Lord and Savior. We were orphans, not enjoying the rights and privileges of sons and daughters of God, and we were slaves to sin. *Even after our salvation, if we haven't yet come into a revelational understanding of God as our good Father—the One who loves us completely and unconditionally—we may still live as orphans or slaves.* But that's not the relationship we were designed to have with the Father.

Living as Orphans or Slaves vs. Living as Heirs

I want you to think for a moment what it was like before you were a Christian. What motivated your decisions then? Was it fear? Fear of what others might think or do? Think about all the things you did that were driven by lust or the fear of missing out. One of the greatest fears we have is the fear of hunger. It's not simply physical hunger or desire that we fear, but we have an irrational fear that, if we don't pursue the things we want, we will never be happy or satisfied. Or if we don't make our future happen, nobody else will. Additionally, the fear of trust is a very real fear. It leads to self-dependence and isolation. According to Romans 8:15, though, for those of us who have "received the Spirit of adoption as sons," we haven't received "the spirit of slavery to fall back into fear." Everything changes when we receive the Spirit, the Spirit of adoption. Everything is supposed to change, that is.

Beloved, sadly, many people come into the Kingdom of God, believing in Jesus, His birth, His death on the cross, and His resurrection, and yet they continue to carry their anxiety, fears, and PTSD. We, like they, can enter the Father's house with our trauma, our mistrust, our self-dependency. *Not having grown yet in our understanding that God no longer sees us as slaves, we continue to live under the rules of the house of slavery from which we were delivered rather than abiding freely in the house of our Father.*

The apostle Paul provided something I believe can better help us get a picture of living as orphans or slave. In Galatians 4:1–5, Paul wrote:

> I mean that the heir, as long as he is a child, is no different from a slave, though he is the owner of everything, but he is under guardians and managers until the date set by his father. In the same way we also, when we were children, were enslaved to the elementary principles of the world. But when the fullness of time had come, God sent forth his Son, born of woman, born under the law, to redeem those who were under the law, so that we might receive adoption as sons.

Paul spoke about an heir, a child in a family who was not old enough to receive the inheritance promised him. He would one day receive it from his guardians on the date his father set for him to receive it. Although technically the heir would become the recipient of everything he inherited, he presently would not be any different than a slave. Think of a very wealthy landowner with a large estate in Ancient Rome. The landowner bequeathed everything to his heir—all his properties, business relationships, and material wealth. Yet within the will, the landowner stipulated that his heir would not have access to the inheritance until that heir came to a certain age of maturity. In the meantime, the guardian or manager would oversee the estate until the day the heir became of age. Legally, the child or heir would possess everything that the father owned, but functionally, the child would live like a slave boy under a guardian or manager. When would the child receive his inheritance and no longer live like a slave? At the appointed age of maturity.

What's the point of Paul's analogy? We all come into the Kingdom by grace through faith.[2] Nobody buys their way into the Kingdom. We can't save ourselves, we can't earn salvation ourselves, and we can't manipulate and receive the salvation of God. We come through the door that is Jesus, by faith and believing, by God's merciful, gracious gift, through which He adopts us into His family and calls us sons and daughters. Once we come into the Kingdom of God, though, it's possible for us to have an inheritance that we can't even fathom or imagine. It's on paper, as it were, written in the Word of God and promised to us. Yet, functionally, we may be living our lives no differently than the slaves we once were, perhaps not doing all the stuff we used to when we were dead in our trespasses and sins. We're living, nonetheless, with a slave mentality or an orphan mentality or an immature mentality. It has nothing to do with the fact that God is not good or that God is playing favorites. It's simply that *our Father has time released His inheritance in our lives, conditioned upon our maturity. There are certain things that we cannot understand or operate in or receive from God until we come into a state of maturity.* And, as long as we remain immature, our lives will look differently than what is already granted us in Christ and documented in God's Word.

Romans 8:17 says that we are "heirs of God and fellow heirs with Christ, provided we suffer with him in order that we may also be glorified with him." Hebrews 5:8 tells us that Jesus's going through trials and tests taught Him obedience. And if we are in Christ, we, too, go through the same, learning obedience like Him through the same means. But what we receive on the other side is the same inheritance that Jesus has received. What is that? Like our Elder Brother, we're going to be raised from the dead. We're going to reign and rule with Him.

Hebrews 1:2 identifies Jesus as "being the heir of all things." *Everything that belongs to God the Father has been given to Christ, and everything that has been given to Christ by the Father belongs to us as well.* But like the example of the landowner, the Father will not release our inheritance into our lives while we are yet immature because we will waste it like the prodigal son did. We'll go out and blow it all on riotous living, making a complete mess of things. But as we allow the Holy Spirit to mature us and to renew our minds and change the way that we see God, see ourselves, and grow in confidence, and when God's Word becomes so deeply implanted in our hearts that it has replaced all the self-dependency, the self-seeking, and the self-protection, all the fear-driven motivation and orphan mentality, we can begin to understand who God is as our Father and get a clear understanding that we are orphaned no more. And that's when we begin to receive what the

Father has for us and walk in the fullness of our inheritance—in the fullness of the Holy Spirit, of power, of strength, of faith, and of confident assurance.

You might say, "Well, how do I know if I'm mature or not?" Here's the true test. What is your first reaction to any given "triggering" circumstance? If your first reaction is to stand in faith or to love, then you're evidencing the "fruit of the Spirit."[3] That is, if your first reaction is love, joy, peace, patience, kindness, gentleness, goodness, or self-control, you're showing the mature fruit of righteous living. On the other hand, if your first reaction is anger, malice, immorality, covetousness, envy, jealousy, lying, selfishness, or condemnation, then you're still living in the place of immaturity.

What's the answer? The answer is we have to yield to the Holy Spirit. And that's an important message for the Church of Jesus Christ. It's time the Church yields to the Holy Spirit and starts to walk in greater obedience to the Father. Only then will we the Church come into a state of maturity as sons and daughters of God, looking and acting more and more like Jesus, our Elder Brother, who is the perfect image of the Father. Why is this important? Because all creation is waiting eagerly "for the revealing of the sons of God."[4] Creation is longing to see men and women who have been redeemed by the blood of Jesus and filled with the Holy Spirit, men and women who finally shift out of orphan and slave mentalities into ways of thinking and operating like mature sons and daughters of God.

> Therefore let us leave the elementary doctrine of Christ and go on to maturity, not laying again a foundation of repentance from dead works and of faith toward God, and of instruction about washings, the laying on of hands, the

resurrection of the dead, and eternal judgment. And this we will do if God permits.

— Hebrews 6:1–3

Remember the Promise of the Helper

God's calling us on to maturity. He is calling us to rise up as sons and daughters and to lay aside the slave and the orphan mentalities that have limited us in the past. We're not slaves in that other house anymore. *God has given us the Spirit of adoption, the indwelling Holy Spirit who is attesting, assuring, and witnessing to the fact that we belong to the Father spiritually, legally, and eternally.* Furthermore, the Holy Spirit in us glorifies Jesus, sanctifies, and matures us so that all the orphan or slave mentalities are eclipsed, removed, and replaced with a grown-up understanding of what it means to be children of God.

I want to close out this chapter underscoring the promise of the Holy Spirit given by Jesus to His disciples in John 14. We discussed this in part in chapter two of this book. But I think it's an important reminder here. In John 14, Jesus told His disciples that He was going to prepare a place for them in His Father's house. In verses 16–17, He made another promise to them, a promise extended to us. Jesus said, "I will ask the Father, and he will give you another Helper to be with you forever, even the Spirit of truth." Then, in verse 18, Jesus pledged, "I will not leave you as orphans; I will come to you."

Notice how Jesus described the One He would give them as "another Helper." The word *Helper* there is transliterated as *paraklētos* in the Greek, which basically refers to One who is called alongside to give aid or comfort. But why did Jesus use the adjective *another* before *Helper*? Because He was promising the disciples and us that this Helper was One of "the same kind." He would ask the Father to send Someone like unto Himself, which we know as the Holy Spirit or, as Jesus referred to Him in verse 17, "the Spirit of truth." It's a beautiful picture of the role the Holy Spirit has in our lives. He is the Helper, the Spirit of truth, sent to us by the Father, and He not only comes alongside us to offer aid and comfort and direction, but Jesus said at the end of John 14:17, the Holy Spirit "dwells with" us and "will be in" us. God can't get any closer than that, dwelling with and living within us. *With God living within us as His temple, we are spiritually in union with Him, and that means we will never, ever be left alone.* And as Romans 8:16 explains, God, by His Holy Spirit within us, "bears witness with our spirit that we are children of God." The Holy Spirit assures us in our spirits of the truth that we are God's sons and daughters. We're not orphans anymore.

One of the prime indicators and inheritances that we receive as children of God is the reality that we no longer have to be driven by fear, that we no longer have to live in self-survival mode, and that we no longer have to be driven or motivated by a desire in and of ourselves to make something happen. Instead, we can be led by the Spirit of God to walk in maturity. Remember, it's the sons of God "who are led by the Spirit of God."[5]

Would you like to know what healed my heart? My heart was healed when the Holy Spirit led me into the truth that God isn't a part-time Father. He doesn't want part-time, weekend custody. The Holy Spirit showed me that the Father isn't Somebody who pops into my life when He wants to and then pops out again. No, I discovered that God the Father is constant. He is everlasting. He is in our lives for the duration, and nothing can separate us from His love.[6]

There is only one thing that can heal your orphaned heart, and that's the Spirit leading you to come into proximity and closeness with the heart of your Heavenly Father. He will heal your heart. He will bring restoration to those places that are broken inside you. You can trust Him because He is everlasting Father. He promises in Hebrews 13:5 that He "will never leave you nor forsake you." This means His physical Presence will never leave you, and He will never withhold His affections from you. You will be orphaned no more.

Prayer

Heavenly Father, I come to You in Jesus's name. I know I've acted as an orphan in the past. I've even wrestled with a slave mentality. I ask that You wash my past, heal my heart, and teach me to trust You. From this day forward, I am no longer an orphan. I am Your child. I'm a part of Your family, and I'm no longer dead in my sins. I'm alive in Christ. Thank You for loving me and saving me.

Jesus, thank You for being the door into the Kingdom and family of God. Help me to be like You. Where I have struggled in the past with thinking and living like an orphan, teach me to live as You lived, as a son.

Holy Spirit, thank You for coming into my life, dwelling in me, and leading me. I surrender today to Your leadership. Thank You that Your very Presence in my life is not only a reminder that I am orphaned no more, but that I have You 24/7, helping me learn more and more how to walk as a child of God.

Reflection

1. What is one moment from your childhood where you can now see God was present even though you felt alone at the time?

2. Who were the "safe harbors" in your life growing up?

3. What did those safe harbors give you that you find yourself still longing for today?

4. When you pray, do you pray more like a child who belongs to the Father or a slave who is afraid of doing something to anger Him?

5. What would you life look like if you didn't live from fear but from sonship or daughterhood?

Chapter 9
Coming to Maturity

Remember what six o'clock meant at the house of my childhood? It meant I'd get to watch *Little House on the Prairie* on TV. If you'll recall, it also meant I'd have to face my stepfather when he walked through the door after a day's work. For about five minutes after he came inside, I could hear the low mutterings of my mom's conversation with my stepfather as I waited upstairs. If he cleared his throat, I was in trouble. But if I heard him respond to Mom's retelling of my mischievous exploits for the day with, "Uh-huh. Uh-huh. Uh-huh," I knew I was in for it.

I grew up in an era where being disciplined included spanking. Back in my day, that was a very common practice in parenting. So, it's no wonder that the worst words I could have heard coming from my mother after I came home from school at 3:30 each weekday afternoon were, "You wait until your dad gets home. He's going to hear about what you've done." I dreaded six o'clock after hearing those words. Even the smile of Charles Ingalls wasn't enough to cheer me up if I knew I was going to get disciplined.

Too many times, my stepdad came upstairs to have a "conversation" with me. He would say, "Your mom told me what happened. She told me what you did. So, what do you think should happen?"

"Dad, I think—I think I've learned my lesson. I think I'm completely sorry. I think this is all overblown, and I want you to know that I'm never gonna do it again," I would try unsuccessfully to delay the inevitable.

And then he would say, "Well, what type of punishment do you think that you deserve?"

Whether it was grounding or spanking or a corrective conversation, the very threat of punishment always produced fear deep in my soul. Now, I believe children should have a healthy reverence for their parents, and loss of privileges, timeouts, and similar disciplinary approaches can help reinforce respect for the authority of parents. But whenever my mom would say, "Your dad will discipline you," my immediate thought was punishment—that he was going to punish me.

The Discipline of the Father

Talking about a father's discipline can cause us to flashback to moments when we were kids and we were punished for doing things that we shouldn't have done. *But when the Bible talks about how the Father disciplines us, its first meaning isn't punishment as much as it is correction and training.* You see, our Heavenly Father puts us through His process of maturity as sons and daughters. Thankfully, our Father doesn't leave us, His children, to our own devices, but He wants to grow us up into full maturity so that we can become who we were called to be, walking in His purposes for our lives. The writer of Hebrews was addressing this process of maturity when he wrote verses 3–11 of chapter 12:

Consider him who endured from sinners such hostility against himself, so that you may not grow weary or faint-hearted. In your struggle against sin you have not yet resisted to the point of shedding your blood. And have you forgotten the exhortation that addresses you as sons? "My son, do not regard lightly the discipline of the Lord, nor be wearied when reproved by him. For the Lord disciplines the ones he loves, and he chastises every son whom he receives." It is for discipline that you have to endure. God is treating you as sons. For what son is there whom his father does not discipline? If you are left without discipline, in which all have participated, then you are illegitimate children and not sons. Besides this, we have had earthly fathers who disciplined us and we respected them. Shall we not much more be subject to the Father of spirits and live? For they disciplined us for a short time as it seemed best to them, but he disciplines us for our good, that we may share his holiness. For the moment all discipline seems painful rather than pleasant, but later it yields the peaceable fruit of righteousness to those who have been trained by it.

The Greek word used here in Hebrews 12 and translated as *discipline* is *paideia,* and its fuller meaning is the act of providing guidance for responsible living, upbringing, training, and instruction, bringing a child to maturity through correction. In fact, the word *paideia* was a huge part of Greek and Greco-Roman cultures as it was used to describe the educational process that young children were taken through so that, by the time they became adults, they were the optimal models of responsible citizenry and leadership. Their discipline or the process wasn't punitive. It was an intentional, educational process that parents would take their children through, and that process would result in creating the best citizens and leaders. The writer of Hebrews was referring to this same process of maturity that the Father leads us through, whereby we become mature sons and daughters, optimal citizens and leaders in the Kingdom of God.

Beloved, God's work in our lives as He relates to us as Father is intentional and formative. It's not punitive. He is training us in righteousness. His very Word, for example, "is profitable for teaching, for reproof, for correction, and for training in righteousness."[1] He hasn't given us a list of rules, perhaps like our earthly fathers may have done, and then said, "Now, I forgave you for all your sin. Go be a good boy, a good girl, and do what I said. If you don't act right, I'll discipline and punish you." That's not what Hebrews 12 is talking about, and that's not really how God responds to us. Let me explain.

Once we are brought into the Kingdom of God and have been born again by His Spirit, we are no longer rebellious children of wrath, dead in our trespasses and sins. Instead, we have entered into a relationship with the Father, and He is leading us, *paideaiing* us, if you will, forming and shaping and instructing and training us in such a way that we become everything He created us to be. Even before the foundations of the world were ever established and even before you and I took our first breaths, He knew us and committed Himself as our Father to train and instruct us. And that discipline of the Father in our lives is invaluable because (1) it demonstrates how committed God is to us and how much He loves us, (2) it shows us we are truly His children, (3) it results in our sharing in His holiness, and (4) it yields "the peaceable fruit of righteousness" if we are trained by it.

God's goal in His discipline is to make us increasingly like His Son, helping us discover who He has made and called us to be. Along the path of grace, the Father leads us, teaches us, and disciplines us, and we grow more confident in His care, intention, and leadership as He does these things. We begin to see what He's calling us to and forming us for. This gives us hope and a vision for our future.

Now, we know discipline and training require endurance on our part. Hebrews 12 affirms that. Most of the things we learn, we don't learn in an instant. We learn through a process of acquiring information and experience over time. I wish it were easy, like putting a USB port into our heads and downloading some new program. Wouldn't that be amazing? But we know that's not how it works. Many people get discouraged after they get saved because they think they should have everything figured out. Not understanding the process, they think, *How come I still have desires to sin? How come I still have an attitude? How come I still use sign language at the person who cuts me off when I'm merging on the highway? Why is it that I get in arguments? What's wrong with me? I thought I was saved.* Maturity doesn't happen in a moment. You can't download everything that you need to know.

Here's what happens to you when you are saved. The Holy Spirit takes up residence in you, but you also have the presence of a sinful nature. This produces a battle inside you, and it's a battle that God wants to teach you how to win. And the way He does it is He takes you through a process. It's a process of uncovering who you are in Christ, your new identity, and it's a process in which God teaches us who we're called to be and what we are destined to become. This is what a father does with a child. "This is who you are. You are a Cummings, and this is how a Cummings acts. This is your story. These are your ancestors. These are the promises, and this is the potential over your life." This is what a father gives to his child, and this is what God wants to give to you.

One of the major issues right now in our culture is people wrestling with the issue of identity. "Who am I? What am I?" And I have deep compassion and deep empathy for people who are struggling with that, and I will tell you that no one really fully knows who they are. It doesn't matter who you are until you find yourself in Christ, until you come face to face with the Heavenly Father, who knows you better than you know yourself. The Father sees the Spirit of the living God dwelling inside you, and He's the One that had purpose for your life before you ever took your first breath. *See, true identity begins when we step into a father-child relationship with God.* This begins the process of maturity. He wants to call you to greatness, He wants to call His Kingdom purposes out of your life, and the way He does that is through instruction, correction, and discipline.

Notice how the writer of Hebrews 12 set up his instruction about God's discipline. His very first statement was to consider Christ, our Elder Brother, so that we don't become "weary or faint-hearted" in the training process. The writer also encourages us to know that the Father disciplines all His children, the very ones He loves. God takes us through, as we talked about dealing with those orphan mentalities that have plagued us and limited us, those orphan mentalities that we grew up in sin. Even if we grew up in church, until the moment that we're born again, we grow up in sin, and in sin, we're spiritual orphans. But Jesus said in John 14, He would not leave us as orphans. In other words, He won't leave us the way He found us, but He will take us on a process of development and maturity. He'll uproot those orphan mentalities and replace them with mature mindsets in Christ Jesus. *Ultimately, God's purpose for you isn't to simply save you, but it's to bring you into the fullness of maturity.*

Listen, nobody has children only to keep them as infants. The goal is that the children grow up and move out someday. In the meantime, we love our children, we teach them, and we prepare them for the day that they leave from the family nest. Nobody gets frustrated with a baby and says, "Would you hurry up and grow up?" No, we love them, and we nurture them. Furthermore, we honor and recognize every step, every phase of the maturing process, because as a parent, we have foresight. We see the potential in them, we identify the gifts and the callings in them, and then we encourage, strengthen, and discipline them, bringing them to a place of maturity. We're only doing that because that's how God responds to us, and like us, His desire is not that we remain saved, little babies. Of course, we are saved, little babies on day one in our relationship with God in Christ, but in year 40 of our walk with God, the Father expects maturity, and He is the One that leads us in that process. In fact, He sets it up for us, using everyday life situations and circumstances in our spiritual formation.

Looking at Galatians 4:19, we can hear the heart of God toward us through the apostle Paul's words: "My little children, for whom I am again in the anguish of childbirth until Christ is formed in you!" Notice the paternal language in this verse. Paul was expressing the apostolic and paternal responsibility he had for the Galatian believers. Like a dad, like a mother, as a parent, he recognized the beginnings of their belief, their faith, and Paul felt their need of his help—to help bring them through the maturity process. That feeling wasn't going to disappear in Paul until he saw Christ fully developed and matured in them. That's the heart of the Father, beloved, for you and me. As we yield to the Father's maturing process and His discipline in our lives, He sets us on a path to walk in the purposes that He established for us. And He will continue, as Paul said, until Christ is fully developed in our lives.

Responding to the Father's Discipline

All true sons and daughters of God will experience the Father's discipline throughout their lives. Because we're His kids, He will challenge some things we do or ways of thinking that need to change. It can happen when we're reading the Bible and come across a verse or passage that convicts us, addressing an area in our thinking or behavior that isn't in alignment with the truth. It can happen when we hear a message at church and, suddenly, say to ourselves, *Uh-oh. I know I'm not living like the pastor says I should be living.* And lest you think we pastors have it all together, let me tell you from personal experience, walking in relationship with the Father has meant having Him correct my attitudes, the way I've looked at situations and even people. He has challenged me in areas of my belief systems and orphan mentalities. This discipline is ongoing in our lives. This process of maturity is not a one-and-done disciplinary measure. Again, it's a continual formation process.

Sometimes, we can think that, if we don't experience correction, then it means we're doing well. The truth is, however, that if we're not receiving correction, we should seriously question whether we're children of God. Don't forget about Hebrews 12. God disciplines the children who are His, the ones He loves. *But just because we hang out in the Father's house doesn't mean we're His children.* I've spent a lot of time in other people's homes, but their parents have never disciplined me. Why? Because I'm not their kid. There are a lot of people who may attend church but have never experienced the correction, the conviction, the discipline, the confrontation of the Father. That should not encourage us. That should concern us because silence is dangerous. *When we experience the discipline of the Lord, it validates our identity, meaning our identity as children of God.* So, if God's not disciplining you and me, if God's not challenging us, one of two things has happened: Either (1) we aren't truly born again and aren't children of God, or (2) we are children of God, but our hearts have become so hardened that we can no longer hear the voice of the Holy Spirit and experience His conviction.

How, then, should we view the discipline of God? How should we respond when it happens to us? Here's how we're supposed to respond to the discipline of the Lord: First and foremost, we're supposed to endure it. We're supposed to let it teach and instruct us. And we're not supposed to discard it or double down in rebellion. Doing that is what leads to the hardening of our hearts until they become so calloused that we can't hear God. That's why the writer of Hebrews says, "If you hear his voice, do not harden your hearts as in the rebellion."[2]

Additionally, Hebrews 12:9 tells us that, seeing we have received and endured the discipline of our earthly fathers, we should even more be subject to our Heavenly Father "and live." *We're called to submit to the process, not buck against the process, not try to minimize the process, but we need to submit to the process because, listen, the process is what brings us into maturity.* It's a process of progress. It's submitting to the process that brings life to us. And we want to recognize that God's goal for our maturation process is good. It's going to produce some very good fruit, peaceable fruit, righteous fruit. We need to know and understand this because so often children don't understand that the disciplines their parents are endeavoring to bring into their young lives are for their good. They don't get that the lesson their mom or dad may be teaching them now is going to pay off for their lives in the long run. We adult children of God sometimes forget that, too—that God has the best intentions for us. His intentions are that we share in His holiness. He wants us to be holy like He is holy. He wants to fully form the nature of His Son in us so that we look more like Jesus than we do ourselves or the world. Can I tell you that either God's nature or your fallen sin nature is going to define every action in your life? It's either God's nature, His holiness—which means we act like Jesus—or it's going to be our fallen, sinful nature. But every decision we make is a decision between which nature we're going to give into.

God's process is to teach us and to train us to respond in partnership with Him. Therefore, our response to the Father's process should be submission and servanthood. We submit to His process, allowing Him to have His way in our lives. And we serve Him throughout the process. When we experience the discipline of the Lord, when God's really zooming in on an area in our lives that's convicting and painful, we're tempted to skirt around it, to avoid the process altogether. Do you know that trying to run away from God's dealings will not produce good in our lives? We may think we're avoiding the pain of conviction and getting around God's process all the while we're running into even more of His dealings and disciplines.

I remember when our son, Jared, was about four years old. We still had those end-of-winter piles of snow in Michigan that were in the process of thawing in the early spring. The children in the middle of our cul-de-sac were running around and sliding down the snowbanks. It was about fifty degrees outside, and our son and some other kids decided they were going to run through the sprinklers as if it were the middle of summer. And Jared wanted to put his swimsuit on so that he could run through the sprinklers with his friends. It was a Saturday, and I was watching something on TV when I said to him, "You're not running through the sprinklers, son, because it's still cold. I know, fifty degrees seems really warm, but if you put on your swimsuit right now and get all wet, you're gonna get cold, and then you're gonna get sick. So, no, you can't turn on the sprinklers and run through them." Of course, he kept on trying to get me to allow him to do what he wanted, but I was firm and said with finality, "Now, go outside and play, but no swimsuit and no sprinklers." He went outside to continue to play, and I went back to watching TV.

A few minutes later, Jane looked through our front door window and called to me, "Lee, you gotta come here and see this!"

Not wanting to be torn away from the TV set yet again, I said, "Why? I'm watching something right now, and—"

"No. Come here. You have to see this now!" she interrupted.

Frustrated, I went to the front door and looked out its window. There, trying to sneak back into our garage, was our son in his snowsuit. He had his hood up and was completely covered in what was supposed to protect him from the cold snow, only he was soaking wet. Here's what he had done. He had heard me tell him that he couldn't run through the sprinkler in his swimsuit because he would get cold and get sick. His solution was to go out into the garage, set the ladder up against the wall, climb up into the tub, get his snowsuit out, and put it on. In his mind, he would keep warm and be able to still run through the sprinklers without getting wet and without getting cold. He also figured that, if he could do all of that and then get back into the garage without getting caught, he could then put everything away without his mother and me knowing. But he happened to look at the front door and saw us looking at him, and he knew he was busted. What do you do as a parent at that moment? I mean this is a four-year-old being innovative and creative, right? What we did was we brought him into the house, and we lovingly disciplined him, all the while laughing and telling him, "Son, that was really ingenious, but you're still getting disciplined, and you're still grounded."

That's an example of how we try to run around God's process. God says, "Don't do this. It isn't good for you," so we try to reason with ourselves as to why it wouldn't be good for us to do. And in that internal dialogue with ourselves, we somehow end up thinking maybe there's a way to get around the "don't do this" of God, finding a "genius" way to do what we want without getting in trouble with God. "I can put my snowsuit on and still be safe and secure, which is what my father was really wanting me to be. I'll protect myself, and it will be okay." Yet we know, like Jared, that we're only trying to get our way and not get in trouble.

Besides showing ourselves how disobedient and willful we are, trying to work around the Father's instruction, we are also revealing that we don't trust the Father's process or that He knows what's best for us. We don't trust that His intentions are good, either, when we try to get around Him. You see, Jesus Himself is our Prototype of what it means to yield to the process of the Father's discipline. In Luke 2:40, we read, "And the child grew and became strong, filled with wisdom. And the favor of God was upon him." The child mentioned here is Jesus. Now, I want you to think about this. This is God in the flesh, Jesus who was fully submitted to the Father, and it says about Him that He "grew and became strong." Growing and becoming strong is a process. Do you know that Jesus, as our Prototype, who goes before us, even though He is and was fully God, still submitted to the Father and to the process? So, lest we think, *Why should I have to go through a formation process?* God points at Jesus, our Elder Brother, and says He went through the process of growth and development.

What's more, as Jesus went through His maturing process, He learned how to partner with the Father in the family business. We see evidence of this in the Gospel of John. On a certain Sabbath, Jesus was walking by the pool of Bethesda, where there were "blind, lame, and paralyzed" lying there.[3] One particular man was lying on the ground "who had been an invalid for thirty-eight years."[4] Jesus healed the man, saying to him, "Get up, take up your bed, and walk."[5] And both the man and Jesus caused quite a stir among the Jews regarding the legality of Jesus healing the man on the Sabbath. We're told, "And this was why the Jews were persecuting Jesus, because he was doing these things on the Sabbath."[6] John 5:17 contains Jesus's response. He said, "My Father is working until now, and I am working." To the Jews, Jesus was not only breaking the Sabbath, but He was even calling God His own Father, and in calling God His Father, Jesus was making Himself equal with God. So, then, Jesus said to them, "Truly, truly, I say to you, the Son can do nothing on his own accord, but only what he sees the Father doing. So whatever the Father does, that the Son does likewise."[7] This is *paideia.* A son watches his father in the family business, and he imitates his father. As the apostle Paul said, "Therefore be imitators of God, as beloved children."[8] That imitation that Paul mentioned as well as what Jesus said about only doing what He saw the Father doing are both examples of *paideia.*

We learn discipline and receive correction and instruction by following in the steps of Jesus, our Elder Brother, who followed in the footsteps of the Father. Like Jesus, we want to do whatever the

Father is doing. It's the partnership with the Father that Jesus modeled for us, and it's the partnership the apostle Paul pointed to in our imitating God. Jesus partnered with the Father, and Jesus became the model and the example that brings many more sons to the Father. As Hebrews 2:10 states, "For it was fitting that he, for whom and by whom all things exist, in bringing many sons to glory, should make the founder of their salvation perfect through suffering." *Jesus was the perfect Son in perfect submission to the Father, going through the process, yielding to the process of the Father and the agenda of the Father, and then in His wake, He is bringing us, His many sons and daughters, to the Father.*

Yes, Jesus is the Prototype for us of submission and obedience to the Father's will, instruction, and process of maturity. Jesus spent a lifetime being trained to please the Father, following in obedience the process of maturity. For one moment, while the crowds were screaming Hosanna, as Jesus entered Jerusalem riding on a donkey's colt, Jesus was thinking about surrendering to the process of His Father as His Son and Servant.[9] While the crowds loved Jesus, He loved the Father. While the crowds and the influencers were promoting Jesus, He was promoting the agenda of the Father. Jesus was so submitted to the Father's will and the Father's agenda that the crowds did not faze him. The gravitational pull of the world was not as strong as the gravitational pull to please the Father.

Beloved, the Father is invested in our lives and in their outcomes. He wants what is best for us, and we will either allow the pull of the world that is undisciplined, that has become dominant in our lives, to influence us and to shape us, or we're going to be like Jesus and submit to the voice of the Father and His discipline. We're either going to please people, to please the world, and to please ourselves, or we're going to please our Father. Even when the crowds in the world and our own sin natures are saying, "We want this. We want to do that," our spirits are being trained and formed to be like Jesus. *Every time we act like Jesus in surrender to the Father's will, we're growing, maturing, and becoming more like Him.* And the more we do that, the more we're able to walk into our destiny, calling, and purpose. This is the goodness of the Father, to train us and discipline us as His children. He doesn't leave us to ourselves and our own devices. He's at work in our lives with our best interests in mind, or more importantly, with His best interests in mind.

I know, at times, the discipline of the Lord and the process of maturity generate more questions than answers. *Religion with its surface relationship with God will produce in you a desire to know the what and the why so that you can still be in control.* But when God is our Father, we trust that He knows the what and the why, even when we don't. When we find our confidence in Him and His kind intentions, that what He is doing is for our good, we yield to His process so that we might share in His holiness, so that our lives might yield the peaceable fruit of righteousness.

God is looking for mature sons and daughters because then we can walk in His purposes in relationship with Him. We can partner with Him to fulfill those purposes. Romans 8:19 says, "For the creation waits with eager longing for the revealing of the sons of God." In other words, you want to know what's wrong? The void that's in our world, the darkness that's there, is awaiting the development and maturation of God's children. The answer to the darkness is the mature light in His children, and it all begins with our trusting God and His process for us to come into that full maturity. An orphan can't trust, and an illegitimate child won't trust. But a child, a son, or a daughter says, "God, I trust You. I wish the cup would pass, and I don't know what kind of cup You'll have me to drink from, but I trust You, and I'll obey."

Perhaps, you've been going through some difficulties, some challenges, some questions, some pain in the process. But if you won't try to circumvent the cup and the process, the Father will bring you to the end, where your trust will be rewarded. Remember that the process is not our doing; it's the Father's doing. We don't discipline ourselves, but today we can choose to come under and to submit to the Father's leadership in our lives. He will produce in us the fruit of righteousness unto maturity, and that's what we want.

Prayer

Father, today, we're choosing to submit to Your process of maturity. We desire Your hand on our lives, leading and directing us. We're submitting to Your process and to Your leadership in our lives. Father, we want to be fully formed, so we don't want to buck against Your process of maturing us, Your process of bringing discipline to bear on our lives. We know You've been dealing with us in certain areas, calling us to repentance, calling us to change. Forgive us for bucking against what You've been asking us to do.

Jesus, we're grateful that You intercede for us still at this moment, as our Elder Brother, as our Lord, as our Savior. Teach us how to trust You.

Holy Spirit, would You draw near to us? Would You give us the grace to submit to You, to yield to You, to want Your way more than our own way? As we yield to You, would You embrace us with the love of the Father, even in the midst of the discipline of the Father?

Lord, we're grateful that You're a tender Father, that You love us. You're not here to break us. You're not here to inflict pain, but You love us so much that You won't let us stay out of Your reach, You won't let us out of Your grip, and we submit to You and say, "Lord, we are here to serve You. We want to be mature sons and daughters that are about our Father's business."

Reflection

1. When you hear the word *discipline,* what memories or emotions does it evoke? How does the Greek word *paidea*—training, formation, guidance, maturation— change the way you understand the discipline of God in your life?

2. What keeps you from fully surrendering to God's maturing process? Pride? Fear? Past experiences? Misunderstanding God's character?

3. How does the idea that God is committed to your full maturity reshape the way you see your life in Christ?

4. What is one step you can take to cooperate with God's maturing process?

Chapter 10
Getting to Know
the Father in Prayer

Only two years had passed since my encounter with God that both helped me to see Him as my Father and changed the trajectory of my life. Then fourteen and faithful in church attendance and very active in youth group, an adult-sized hunger burned within my soul to know God, to know Him like my grandparents and others seemed to know Him.

Having become passionate in my pursuit of God the Father, I got even more fired up when someone gave me a gift that I felt was going to help me in my quest. The book was titled *Could You Not Tarry One Hour?* and was written by Larry Lea. The title was based on Jesus's question to Peter in the garden of Gethsemane: "Could you not watch with Me one hour?"[1] The book itself contained the Lord's Prayer broken down into an outline created to be used as a tool for helping readers pray for one hour, which was something I was finding difficult to do at that time in my life. Inspired by the book and desiring to know God more, I committed myself to get up early to pray each day for an hour before school.

I remember the first night I prepared myself for early morning prayer, intent on using Lea's book to help extend my prayer time. Self-assured and determined, I set my alarm for five o'clock. I went to bed convinced I was going to get up early and go after God. I had all kinds of high-minded ideas of what was going to happen when I got up for prayer. It's embarrassing to admit now, but in my youthfulness, I thought I was going to impress God by my getting up so early to seek Him and to show Him how much I wanted to know Him. You can only imagine how disappointed with myself I was the next morning when the alarm went off and I hit the snooze button. I'd like to be able to say I got up when the alarm sounded ten minutes later, but I didn't. I hit snooze again. Let's just say I hit the snooze button enough times to make me miss having any prayer time with God. I finally rolled out of bed with only enough time to get myself ready and off to school.

All that day, I carried guilt and shame around like a weighted backpack strapped to me. I kept on comparing myself in my mind to Peter, James, and John in the garden during Jesus's agony— unable to pray for an hour. But that wasn't a fair comparison at all because I couldn't even get myself out of bed to show up for prayer. At least the three disciples-turned-apostles had been able to go with Jesus to the garden. I remember thinking, *God, I've failed You. I can't believe that I couldn't even get up out of my bed to pray this morning. I'm terrible, but I promise that tomorrow—tomorrow, I'm going to do it! I'm going to get up and pray at five o'clock.*

Tomorrow came, and you can guess what I did. I didn't wake up in time. The alarm buzzed. I hit snooze. The alarm buzzed. I hit snooze. This became my early morning pattern for the next few days. But then, one morning, I finally got up at five and was very proud of myself as I took the steps down to our dank, dark, and scary basement with our big monster boiler. I was afraid to be down there alone to talk to God, but I went ahead and stayed, sitting on the little futon we had down there. What happened over the next few minutes wasn't necessarily what I had imagined, but at least I was down there at a little after five, and my heart, soul, mind, and strength were set to pray for an hour.

I opened my Bible. I read about a chapter, and then I started to use my notes from Lea's outline to help me pray through the Lord's Prayer. I got through that and then took out a prayer list I had made of people and situations I knew needed God's help and intervention. When I got done, I looked at my watch. Eight minutes had passed. And all I could see in my mind's eye was the convicting title of Lea's book, *Could You Not Tarry One Hour?*

After finally making it downstairs early in the morning to pray, I wasn't about to let a little discouragement send me away disappointed in myself again. I hadn't awakened that early for nothing. I was going to tarry for an hour, no matter what. So, I started praying for everyone and everything. I mean, I prayed for the neighbors' dogs, their cats, the monster boiler—you name it, I probably prayed for it. I looked at my watch again sure I had been praying for over an hour, but only eleven total minutes had elapsed.

Certain God was upset with me, I felt complete and utter defeat. And it was all based on a presupposition that I had—that prayer was me proving my worth to God and convincing Him by my eloquence, my discipline, or my righteousness that He should give me what I asked for. I didn't understand then that *prayer is about relationship and not performance.*

I continued to struggle in my prayer life with the guilt I felt for not being able to pray for long. Something soon changed after I went on a three-day youth retreat in Muskegon, Michigan. A man whose name I can't remember ministered to us there. He taught on prayer, and he said something that radically changed my perspective by changing my presupposition. He said, *"God doesn't just tolerate you. God actually loves you. And prayer is all about you spending time with Him because He wants to spend time with you."*

In that moment, something inside clicked instantly, and I realized I had been "doing" prayer all wrong. *Prayer is not about how well I pray or how long I pray—how strong or weak I am in prayer. Prayer is about relationship with God my Father.* It's in prayer where the Holy Spirit unveils the Father's heart to me. It's in prayer where I reveal myself to the Father, unashamed and unafraid of rejection. And it's in prayer where I encounter Him and grow in my understanding of who I am, whose I am, and who He is.

Prayer: It's About Relationship

The psalmist David described our longing for God "as a deer" panting for water.[2] Indeed, our souls are thirsty for Him, and yet we spend much of our lives testing, trying, pursuing, and drinking other things that we think will satisfy us, but they only leave us with greater thirst. Some of those things aren't necessarily bad. They simply were never meant to quench our soul's thirst.

John Piper used starvation, rather than thirst, as the metaphor for longing. He explained, "We are all starved for the glory of God, not self. No one goes to the Grand Canyon to increase self-esteem. Why do we go? Because there is greater healing for the soul in beholding splendor than there is in beholding self."[3]

Too much of our lives is spent looking upon our own reflections or beholding the fractured images of other fallen people. Thankfully, God invites us to come to Him and behold Him, which is essentially what prayer is. We come before God in relationship, in response to His invitation to see and know Him. And it's in that moment of beholding our Heavenly Father and learning about Him that we experience the one thing meant to satisfy our panting, starving, thirsting souls—and that's Him. *All our desire, hunger, and thirst are satiated in prayer, in reading His Word and worshiping Him as we behold Him.*

Prayer is not some religious obligation, ritual, or activity we do only in our darkest moments or for brownie points with our Maker. It's not some SOS we throw up to the heavens with the hope that God may rescue us or meet our need. *Prayer is meant to be our inhale and our exhale.* It's meant to be an intrinsic part of our lives with the Father, in growing in our knowledge of Him. It's also where we're supposed to find life—in the place of beholding God our Father, because God Himself is life.

Prayer is about relationship with Him. As we pray, we give God what He wants, which is our attention. In return, we get what we need. We get the living water Jesus spoke about to the Samaritan woman at the well. Their conversation is depicted in John 4:7–26. Jesus told her, "Whoever drinks of the water that I will give him will never be thirsty again," because the water that Jesus gives "will become in him a spring of water welling up to eternal life."[4]

We can experience God to the degree that we desire Him. Jesus Himself said, "Blessed are those who hunger and thirst for righteousness, for they shall be satisfied."[5] Who gets satisfied or filled? Those who are hungry and thirsty. And as our thirst increases, so does our encounter or experience with Him. If we respond to His invitation to drink of the water He offers us, then we come to Him, and in the place of prayer and encounter, He gives us what will satisfy our thirst.

Beloved, I cannot emphasize this truth enough—God desires to know you, the real you, even more than you desire to know Him. I'm not saying that God doesn't know you already. The Scripture tells us that He is omniscient. He knows all. He knows our thoughts afar off.[6] He knows what we need before we even ask for it.[7] And He even knows the number of hairs we have on our heads.[8] Put simply: He knows us. But He wants to hear about us from us. More specifically, He wants the kind of knowledge that comes from you willingly drawing near to Him and openly inviting Him into your deepest realms and thoughts. In return, by the Holy Spirit who dwells within us, He shows us the deep places, emotions, and wisdom of Himself. This is true *intimate knowledge.* He wants you to come into the secret place, shut the door behind you, and listen to you tell Him all about everything—about your fears, your hopes, your dreams, your successes, your failures. And then, only as a father can do, He wants to share His comfort, leadership, and eternal perspective on those things that bring you into partnership with Him as a mature son or daughter. He is not looking to keep you immature and childish but to mature you by the time you spend with Him. The more His heart and perspective become yours, the more your maturity level increases, and you are enabled to walk in your full inheritance.

You know, we spend a lot of time trying to convince God to hear our prayers. They tend to sound like this, "Father, I know You're busy running the universe. I know You have a lot on Your plate right now, and there are many people here on Earth who are much more worthy than I to receive Your time, affection, and attention. But would You give me 15 seconds in my darkest moment as I lob up this prayer to You, and would You help me out?" We think that we're inconveniencing God, but He truly loves it when we come to Him for help in time of trouble or simply because we want to draw close to Him. Amazingly, when we do draw close to Him, we can begin to feel the warmth of His gaze upon our hearts and the love He has for us. It's in moments like these where we can begin to worship Him and love Him back with the love He's given us. After all, it takes God to love God.

Prayer goes from drudgery to a lifestyle when we receive and embrace the revelation that, as much as we want to know God, God desires for us to open up our hearts and lives to Him in full disclosure even more. And He longs to reveal Himself to us through our reading His Word and listening to His Holy Spirit in us as He continues to speak to us about Himself, about our identity as His son or daughter, and about His great love for us.

Prayer: It's About Love

The prophet Hosea declared, "I don't want your sacrifices—I want your love; I don't want your offerings—I want you to know me."[9] Hosea was the first of the minor prophets, prophesying primarily to the Northern Kingdom about their unfaithfulness and idolatry. God was speaking very clearly through the prophet, telling Israel that He wanted their love and He wanted them to know Him. It should blow our minds that the God of the universe who created everything, who is way beyond human ability to comprehend or apprehend, doesn't merely acknowledge our existence or provide for us because He has to. He truly wants us to love Him, and He wants to lavish His love upon us. He hasn't given us His Word as a rulebook, beloved, but He has given it to us as a love letter. He has given it to us as a massive formal invitation, not to a religion or a behavioral modification program, but an invitation to know and love Him deeply and intimately as our Father.

When you pray out of obligation, when you pray trying to convince God you're worthy of His approval and answer, you're altogether missing what prayer is about. You're coming at prayer and relating to God with the same presupposition I did—that prayer was about performance, that if you do it well, you're going to be approved, but if you don't do it well, then you're going to be condemned. Listen, you will never be consistent in prayer if it's up to your performance. The truth is this: *Coming to God with a performance mentality in prayer is closer to witchcraft than it is to biblical prayer.* Witchcraft is saying some type of incantation to get what you want. If you get it right, you get the right formula, you can manipulate the spirits of the universe to do what you want them to do. That's what witchcraft says. That's not prayer. Prayer is surrendering yourself to God who loves you far more than you love Him. And if your heart is convinced of the truth that God invites you to pray and come to know Him, because He loves you, then prayer becomes exhilarating. You find yourself running to Him as your Father, assured of His love and embrace.

Jesus said in John 14:21, "He who loves me will be loved by my Father, and I will love him and manifest myself to him." What did Jesus mean? He meant that, if you love Jesus, the Father loves you, and He will make Himself known, He "will manifest" Himself to you. That's a promise from the Bible for you. A lot of times we think God is hiding from us. But the reality is God is hiding Himself *for* us. And He says, "Come and find Me. Come deeper." One psalmist wrote, "Deep calls to deep at the roar of your waterfalls."[10] God's voice is epitomized in the Scriptures like the sound of waterfalls, and here the psalmist was talking about the deepest longing inside is being called to from someplace outside this world, outside daily experience, outside weakness, outside limitations. And listen to me, saint, God's deep is calling to the deep inside you. It's love expressed in longing and desire as God's longing for you draws you into a longing for Him—to know Him and to be known by Him. See prayer is not our idea. We often think that we came up with it, but prayer is God's idea.

Prayer: It's About Unmasking

God's gift to us is this beautiful activity called prayer. God calls us to pray. He wants us to pray. And the reality is He is waiting for us to pray. Jesus, when He was teaching on prayer in Matthew 6, He turned the tables over on the religious who thought they had prayer all figured out. They thought that their prayers, their eloquence, their righteousness as Pharisees and Sadducees controlled everything. I like to use the image of a spiritual casino where the house always wins, and the Pharisees and Sadducees thought they were the house. They saw themselves as the casino owners, but Jesus turned the tables over on their concept of being owners of the house. In Matthew 6:5–8, Jesus said to His disciples,

> When you pray, you must not be like the hypocrites. For they love to stand and pray in the synagogues and at the street corners that they may be seen by others. Truly, I say to you, they have received their reward. But when you pray, go into your room and shut the door and pray to your Father who is in secret. And your Father who sees in secret will reward you. And when you pray, do not heap up empty phrases as the Gentiles do, for they think that they will be heard for their many words. Do not be like them, for your Father knows what you need before you ask Him.

Isn't it crazy that God knows everything that we need, yet He still wants us to ask Him? *God, why? If You know what I need, why not give it to me?* Because God wants to be more than some vending machine. *God wants to be your Father. He wants relationship. He wants the joy of us asking and then showing to us His wisdom and His power and His beauty by providing those things to us.* When He was saying not to be like the hypocrites, He was talking about someone who wears masks like an actor. That word *hypocrite* in the Greek is referring to the masked actor. In Greek theater, actors who were acting out Greek tragedies or plays would wear different masks suited for the different roles they were playing. If they were a villain, they would wear a villain mask. They had different masks that they wore. So what Jesus was saying was, "Don't wear your masks, and don't assume a role when you pray." God isn't looking for you to play a role, and He isn't looking for you to know some script. He doesn't want us to act fake in His Presence. He wants you to drop the mask because He wants to see and hear the authentic you.

If we're honest, we wear different masks when we pray. I believe there are three particular masks that I think we find ourselves wearing in prayer. They represent roles that we think we have to play when it comes to prayer. My hope is that, by exposing them, we can learn to drop them and be free from them. *Number one is the mask of formality.* This is religious traditions and cold externality. When we wear this mask in prayer, we say all the right things, but our hearts aren't really in it. We may pray out of religious tradition, but it isn't relational. We pray King James prayers, "Oh, Thou Lord of the universe," we may pray. Do you talk like that? No. We learn that in religion. God wants us to drop the mask of religious formality.

The second mask we may wear while praying is the mask of familiarity. Familiarity is when we take God lightly or are disrespectful in His Presence or in our approach to Him. We're kind of flippant in prayer. It's like, "Hey, Jesus, You know, You're my best friend. You're my homeboy." There is a difference between fear and holy reverence. When we come into the Presence of God, we can put on a mask of familiarity with God, trying to bring God down to our level. But, beloved, God is not at our level. He invites us to behold Him and to know Him, but we should stand in awe of Him when we approach Him.

The third mask that we need to drop is the mask of inferiority. We wear this mask when we relate to God out of fear and are afraid of approaching God. When we're wearing this mask, our prayers can sound like, "God, listen, I know I haven't been to church in a decade. I know that I've really messed things up. I know that You know what a terrible person I am, and that You probably don't want to hear from me, but if You will do this for me, I promise You that I'll never sin again." But God doesn't want us to hide behind our inferiority when we pray. He wants us to remove the masks and draw close to Him as our authentic selves— no pretense, no hiding, no falsehood.

See, ultimately, prayer is us wading out into the depths of pursuit to know God the Father. It is us wading out past our comfort zones. We keep pushing and pushing and going deeper and deeper. And that's what prayer is. The lifestyle of prayer is us pursuing, walking deeper, wading out into the depths to know Father. Romans 11:33 says, "Oh, the depth of the riches and wisdom and knowledge of God! How unsearchable are his judgments and how inscrutable his ways!" God wants to know you, and He wants you to know Him. He is inviting you to come out deeper. And as you step into knowing Him day by day, here is what happens: *God's nature, His essence, His Word, and His Presence wash over you like waves that begin to erode away your fears.* As Psalm 42:7 says, "All your breakers and your waves have gone over me." All His breakers smash like waves on the shore that begin to change the coastline.

The coastline of your heart and of your soul and of your spirit begin to get eroded. Your independence, your hopelessness, your fatherlessness, your pursuit of other things, your satisfaction with the things of this world begin to be eroded as you go deeper into the tall waves and the billows and the breakers of God's nearness to you in prayer.

Sometimes, we need our paradigms of who God is to be broken. That's what must happen for us to begin to know who God the Father truly is. It's in prayer where we'll find Him waiting for us, ready to reveal Himself to us and heal the shattered shards of a broken father image we have projected onto Him. The place of drawing near to Him becomes the Living Room in which we are no longer afraid to approach Him because we have become confident in His love for us. It's in prayer where we'll behold and discover more of who He is and what it is that He has always intended for us. It's in prayer where we drop our masks, come out from behind the trees we've hidden behind for years. It's in prayer where we'll come into close proximity with His Person and His passion for us. Andrew Murray in *The Secret of Adoration* said:

> Take time. Give God time to reveal Himself to you. Give yourself time to be silent and quiet before Him, waiting to receive, through the Spirit, the assurance of His presence with you, His power working in you.
>
> Take time to read His Word as in His presence, that from it you may know what He asks of you and what He promises you. Let the Word create around you, create within you a holy atmosphere, a holy heavenly light, in which your soul will be refreshed and strengthened for the work of daily life.[11]

Prayer

And so, Father, with our hands lifted, we hear the deep of Your heart calling to the deep of ours. Your voice is like the sound of waterfalls, and Your love, goodness, tenderness, kindness, Word, and Presence are washing over us like waves and billows. Father, we thirst for You as the deer pants for the water. God, You're the only thing that can satisfy us. The essence of who we are was meant to be filled with more of You, to know You, to walk with You, not to be religious people who know how to pray externally with our hearts pursuing other things, thinking they will satisfy us, Father. No, every single day, we are meant to drink deeply from the wells of who You are, Father. And to think that You wait for us in the place of prayer, in our secret place, on our chair, on our couch, in our bedroom, in our living room, in our car, in our office.

Father, we say yes to your invitation into the deep. May we no longer see You through the broken reflections of our experiences. From here on out, we want to know You as Father so that everything that needs to be changed in us is changed. Make us like You, Father, so that we can glorify You in all we say and do, in Jesus's name. Amen.

Reflection

1. How does the Father's wanting to spend time with you change your approach to prayer and also to your understanding of His heart toward you?

2. Have you found yourself trying to hide behind a mask in your prayer life? Have you ever felt the need to use a

script to talk to God? In what ways will the discussion on unmasking affect your future prayer time with God?

3. How can you ensure your prayer time is more surrendering yourself to God rather than attempting to manipulate Him or get Him to do what you want Him to do?

4. What specific areas of your life (e.g., independence, hopelessness, fatherlessness, distrust, fear, etc.) do you want the breakers and waves of God's nearness to transform?

Notes

1. Leaving Behind the Fractured Image

1. Ryan King, "Exclusive: GOP Lawmakers Push Bill Touting Dads for Father's Day—and Calling out Crisis of 1 and 4 Kids Growing up without one," New York Post, June 15, 2025. https://nypost.com/2025/06/15/us-news/gop-lawmakers-push-bill-touting-dads-for-fathers-day-and-calling-out-crisis-of-1-and-4-kids-growing-up-without-one/?utm_source=chatgpt.com/.
2. King, "Exclusive: GOP Lawmakers Push Bill."
3. King, "Exclusive: GOP Lawmakers Push Bill."
4. Jack Brewer, "Fatherlessness in the National Capital Region," AFPI (America First Policy Institute), August 25, 2022, https://www.americafirstpolicy.com/issues/20220825-fatherlessness-in-the-national-capital-region/.
5. Brewer, "Fatherlessness in the National Capital Region."
6. WifiTalents Team, "Fatherless Household Statistics," WifiTalents, June 2, 2025, https://wifitalents.com/fatherless-household-statistics/?utm_source=chatgpt.com/.
7. The statistics listed in bullets are taken from WifiTalents Team, "Fatherless Household Statistics," WifiTalents, June 2, 2025, https://wifitalents.com/fatherless-household-statistics/?utm_source=chatgpt.com/.
8. See 1 Tim 2:14.
9. Bishop Robert Barron, *Letter to a Suffering Church: A Bishop Speaks on the Sexual Abuse Crisis,* (Park Ridge, IL: Word on Fire, 2019), 72.
10. Gen 1:26.
11. 1 John 3:1 NKJV.
12. A.W. Tozer, *The Knowledge of the Holy,* (New York: HarperCollins, 1978), 1.

2. Looking to the Perfect Image

1. Col 1:15.
2. Col 2:9.
3. See John 14:1–3.
4. John 14:4.
5. John 14:5.
6. John 14:8.

7. John Piper, "I Am the Way, the Truth, and the Life," desiringGod, March 23, 2012, https://www.desiringgod.org/messages/i-am-the-way-the-truth-and-the-life/.

8. Alexander McLaren, D. D., Litt. D., "Faith in God and Christ," *Expositions of Holy Scripture, St. John Chapters I–XIV,* vol. X, (Grand Rapids, MI: Wm. B. Eerdmans Publishing Co., 1944), 260.

9. See John 12:27–36; 17:1–8.

10. Matt 6:6 NKJV.

11. R.C. Sproul, "Our Father," The Lord's Prayer, Ligonier.org, June 5, 2025, https://learn.ligonier.org/articles/our-father/. R.C. Sproul explains, "The German scholar Joachim Jeremias has argued that in almost every prayer that Jesus utters in the New Testament, He addresses God as Father. Jeremias notes that this represents a radical departure from Jewish custom and tradition. Though Jewish people were given a lengthy number of appropriate titles for God in personal prayer, significantly absent from the approved list was the title 'Father.' To be sure, the Jews would use the term 'Father' indirectly by addressing God as the Father of people, but never by way of a direct address, in which the person praying addressed God in personal terms as 'Father.'"

12. Rabbi Jason Sobel, "The Lord's Prayer and You," Fusion with Rabbi Jason, https://www.fusionglobal.org/connections/lords-prayer/.

13. See Phil 2:1–11.

14. See Heb 2:10–18 for how Jesus serves as our Elder Brother.

3. Returning to the Father

1. See Luke 15:1–2.
2. Luke 15:4.
3. Luke 15:6.
4. Luke 15:8.
5. Luke 15:9.
6. Luke 15:7, 10.
7. Luke 15:14.
8. Luke 15:15–16.
9. Luke 15:20.
10. Luke 15:21.
11. Luke 15:25–28.
12. Luke 15:28.
13. Luke 15:31–32.
14. Timothy Keller, *The Prodigal God: Recovering the Heart of the Christian Faith,* (New York: Penguin House, 2008), 42.
15. Keller, *Prodigal God,* 41–42.

16. See Rom 8:9, 14.

4. Belonging to the Father

1. Abraham Maslow, "A Theory of Human Motivation," *Psychological Review,* 50(4), 370–396.
2. Charles McDermid, "How Money Motivates Men," *Business Horizons,* 3(2), 93–98.
3. Roy F. Baumeister & Mark R. Leary, "The Need to Belong: Desire for Interpersonal Attachments as a Fundamental Human Motivation," *Psychological Bulletin,* 117(3), 497–529.
4. Vivek H. Murthy, MD, *Together: The Healing Power of Human Connections in a Sometimes Lonely World,* (HarperWave: New York, 2020), 8.

5. Adopted by the Father

1. John 3:16.
2. Rom 8:15; Gal 4:6.
3. See Rom 5:5.
4. See 1 John 3:9; 1 Pet 1:23.
5. Abraham E. Fenton, *The Greatest Offer,* (Big Flats, NY: Furrow Press, 2014), 29–30.
6. 2 Pet 1:4.
7. See Eph 2:19; 1 Tim 3:15.
8. John 14:2.
9. See Phil 4:19.
10. Heb 13:6.
11. Mark 1:10–11.
12. Matt 4:2–3.
13. 2 Tim 3:17.
14. John 16:13.
15. Heb 12:5–6.

6. Identity Defined and Value Affirmed

1. John 3:2.
2. John 3:3.
3. John 3:4.
4. Jennifer Wallace, *Never Enough: When Achievement Culture Becomes Toxic— and What We Can Do About It,* (New York: Portfolio/Penguin, 2023), back

cover. "Drawing on interviews with families, educators, and an original survey of nearly 6,000 parents, she exposes how the pressure to perform is not a matter of parental choice but baked in to our larger society and spurred by increasing income inequality and dwindling opportunities. As a result, children are increasingly absorbing the message that they have no value outside of their accomplishments, a message that is reinforced by the media and greater culture at large."

5. See Phil 3:20.
6. See 1 Pet 2:11.

7. Vulnerability Protected

1. See Song 8:4.
2. Gen 1:31.
3. Gen 2:9.
4. Gen 2:16–17.
5. Gen 2:8.
6. Gen 2:17.
7. Matt 23:27.
8. See Isa 64:6 NKJV.
9. Gen 3:9.
10. Gen 3:10.
11. Gen 3:21.
12. See Ps 68:5.
13. John 14:6.
14. See Heb 4:16.

8. Orphaned No More

1. See Mirielle Corbier's discussion of this in "Divorce and Adoption as Familial Strategies" in Beryl Rawson's *Marriage Divorce and Children in Ancient Rome* (Oxford: Oxford University Press, 1996).
2. See Eph 2:8.
3. Gal 5:22–23.
4. Rom 8:19.
5. Rom 8:14.
6. See Rom 8:35.

9. Coming to Maturity

1. 2 Tim 3:16.
2. Heb 3:15.
3. John 5:3.
4. John 5:5.
5. John 5:8.
6. John 5:16.
7. John 5:19.
8. Eph 5:1.
9. Matt 21:6–11.

10. Getting to Know the Father in Prayer

1. Matt 26:40 NKJV.
2. Ps 42:1.
3. John Piper, *Seeing and Savoring Jesus Christ,* (Wheaton, IL: Crossway, 2004), 15.
4. John 4:14.
5. Matt 5:6.
6. See Ps 139:2.
7. See Matt 6:8.
8. See Luke 12:7.
9. Hosea 6:6 TLB.
10. Ps 42:7.
11. Taken from Andrew Murray's *The Secret of Adoration,* and posted on https://www.stmaryalexandria.org/wp-content/uploads/2018/11/Adoration-Take-time.pdf/.

Acknowledgments

There are several people whom I want to acknowledge as vital to this book becoming a reality.

Edie Mourey, you are a gifted writer, editor, and prophetic voice all knotted up together. I am grateful for all your help and ideas.

Sean Downs, your eye for detail and commitment to help me publish the message that I burn with has brought this from a concept to reality.

Krista Kennedy, the best personal and executive assistant on the planet, you help me organize my life so that these books can get written.

Wayne Drain, thank you for your prophetic encouragement to write this message and allow myself to be vulnerable so that another generation can gain from my personal journey.

The whole staff of Radiant Church and Radiant Network, your faith and support mean more than you know.

And as always, the one person on this round ball planet that means more to me than anyone can fathom, Jane, you're my wife, friend, partner, champion, and witness to my journey of knowing God as my Father. He knew this young, twenty-year-old man would need a helpmate of exceptional character and grace, so God gave me you. If ever I doubt His love for me, I only have to look at you, and my faith is restored.

About the Author

Lee Cummings is the founding and senior leader of Radiant Church. Lee and his wife, Jane, started Radiant in 1996 in a high school auditorium in Richland, Michigan, a rural community in the outskirts of Kalamazoo. Since then, Radiant Church has grown to reach thousands of people in several locations. Radiant is a praying and worshiping church that is relentlessly leading people to become fully formed disciples of Jesus Christ living on mission together.

Since 2016, Lee has also served as the founder and overseer of the Radiant Network, a family of churches and leaders who share a common vision for growing the Kingdom.

Lee and Jane currently reside in Kalamazoo. They were married in 1992 and have three grown children, two sons-in-law, one daughter-in-law, and five grandchildren.

Also by Lee Cummings

In His House: Plant Your Life Where God Designed It to Thrive

An Overview of Why Israel Matters

Take Heed, Watch & Pray: Overcoming Deception in the Last Days

Give No Rest! A Renewed Commitment to Pursue God's Presence in Prayer and Worship in the American Church

School of the Spirit: Living the Holy Spirit-Empowered Life

Be Radiant: Becoming Who God Meant You to Be

SCAN FOR BOOKS, COURSES,
BLOGS, PODCASTS, AND MORE

@LEEMCUMMINGS